SIEG TRAVERS

THERAPEUTIC LANDSCAPES

The Ultimate Guide to Landscaping For Your Home,
Discover Ideas and Tips on How You Can Plan, Design, Build
and Plant to Create Your Own Beautiful Garden

Descrierea CIP a Bibliotecii Naționale a României
SIEG TRAVERS
THERAPEUTIC LANDSCAPES. The Ultimate Guide to Landscaping For Your Home, Discover Ideas and Tips on How You Can Plan, Design, Build and Plant to Create Your Own Beautiful Garden / Sieg Travers – Bucharest: Editura My Ebook, 2021
   ISBN

SIEG TRAVERS

THERAPEUTIC LANDSCAPES
The Ultimate Guide to Landscaping For Your Home,
Discover Ideas and Tips on How You Can Plan, Design, Build
and Plant to Create Your Own Beautiful Garden

My Ebook Publishing House
Bucharest, 2021

CONTENTS

Planning The Home Landscape 7

The Base Plan 10

Planning For Your Needs 19

Studying The Site 21

Landscaping Materials 30

Placing Your Plants 41

Choosing And Planting Your Plants 45

Landscape Construction 120

Terracing 124

Backyard Ponds 130

Landscaping For Energy Savings 141

PLANNING THE HOME LANDSCAPE

A landscape which is designed properly is a source of enjoyment for the entire family, it enhances a community and adds to the resale value of your property. Landscape design involves much more than placing trees, shrubs and other plants on the property. It is an art which deals with conscious arrangement or organization of outdoor space for human satisfaction and enjoyment.

Some of its major goals include:

❑ Organizing and developing the site for maximum use and pleasure.

❑ Creating a visual relationship between the house and the site.

❑ Reducing landscape maintenance to a practical level.

Americans spend tremendous amounts of money landscaping their businesses, homes, streets, parks, schools, etc. Much of this money is wasted, however, because of little or no planning. People cannot understand *how* to landscape until they know *why* they landscape.

There are several reasons why people landscape: some think it improves the appearance of their place; others like to grow plants; still others just want their place to look pretty. Too often these landscapes dominate rather than serve. Masses of plants or other materials in the landscape may take up a large portion of the space and leave little room for people.

So how does the designer arrange space so that people will find it useful, beautiful, meaningful and functional? His methods include:

❑ Observing and analyzing the habits of the people who will be using the space, including their needs, desires and how much space each of their activities requires.

❑ Studying past landscaping methods.

❑ Surveying available materials to solve design requirements.

❑ Analyzing the environment of the site including the view in and around the site. The ecology of the site should be carefully analyzed since it is important in determiningthe design.

Not all landscaping improves the appearance of a building. The work of an insensitive designer can subdue a building, conceal important features or contradict the architect's intent.

Good landscape design can significantly improve the building's appearance by adding warmth, liveability and personality. It can also relate a building to its site and environment and give it the desired degree of dominance.

Growth and change separate landscape designs from other arts. Most works of art such as architecture, sculpture and painting look their best when new. Landscape designs, however, are at their worst when new and improve with age. A well-designed landscape will seldom look the same any two months of the year.

The urge to begin planting immediately is almost overwhelming. Whether you are landscaping a newly-built home or redesigning an existing landscape, the results will be much more satisfying if you plan first. If you follow the steps provided in this manual you can produce a plan that will result in a satisfying landscape.

THE BASE PLAN

If a landscape is a picture, it must have a canvas. This canvas is the lawn. Upon the lawn, the artist paints with tree and bush and flower as the painter does upon his canvas with brush and pigments. The opportunity for artistic composition and design is nowhere so great as in the landscape garden, because no other art has such a limitless field for the expression of its emotions.

The making of a good and spacious lawn, then, is the very first practical consideration in a landscape. The lawn provided, the gardener conceives what is the dominant and central feature in the place, and then throws the entire premises into subordination to this feature. In home grounds this central feature is the house. To scatter trees and bushes over the area defeats the fundamental purpose of the place, - the purpose to make every part of the grounds lead up to the home and to accentuate its homelikeness.

It is desirable to have a definite plan on paper for the location of the leading features of the place. These features are the residence, the out buildings, the walks and drives, the service areas, the border planting, flower-garden, and vegetable-garden. It should not be expected that the map plan can be followed in every detail, but it will serve as a general guide.

To begin, you will need to draw a base plan to scale. For most properties a scale of 1/8"=1' is workable; for small properties or a particular area of a larger development 1/4"=1' may be better.

Graph paper with lines indicating a particular scale may also be helpful.

You should include all the major features of your property on your drawing such as existing walks, terraces, outbuildings, trees, shrubs, drives, property lines, easements, utilities, etc.

After you have prepared the base plan you can place tracing paper or tissue paper over the original plan to sketch possible ideas and solutions to your landscape needs and problems.

Steps For Drawing The Base Plan

SUGGESTED SYMBOLS

———— PROPERTY LINE	+ WATER SPIGOT
— — — — CITY EASEMENT	Ⓖ GAS METER
——— ——— SEWER LINE	Ⓦ WATER METER
············ ELECTRIC LINE	Ⓕ FIRE HYDRANT
——— - - ——— WATER LINE	Ⓐ AIR CONDITIONING UNIT
✦ TELEPHONE POLE	

EXISTING TREE   EXISTING SHRUBS   STEEP SLOPE

WINDOW   DOOR

SLIDING GLASS DOOR   HOUSE   ROOF LINE-OVERHANG

Step One: Indicate the compass directions in relation to the house by drawing an arrow (N->) pointing north. You may also want to show the direction of the rising sun. In winter, the sun rises a little south of east and sets a little south of west. In summer, the sun rises somewhat north of east and sets somewhat north of west.

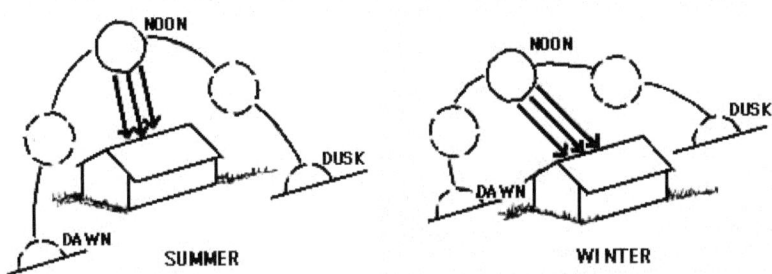

SEASONAL SUN ANGLES WHICH WILL
AFFECT THE DESIGN OF THE LANDSCAPE

SUMMER   WINTER

Step Two: Measure each property line and record the measurement on a rough skech. If a plot plan of the lot is available, you can use the dimensions shown on it.

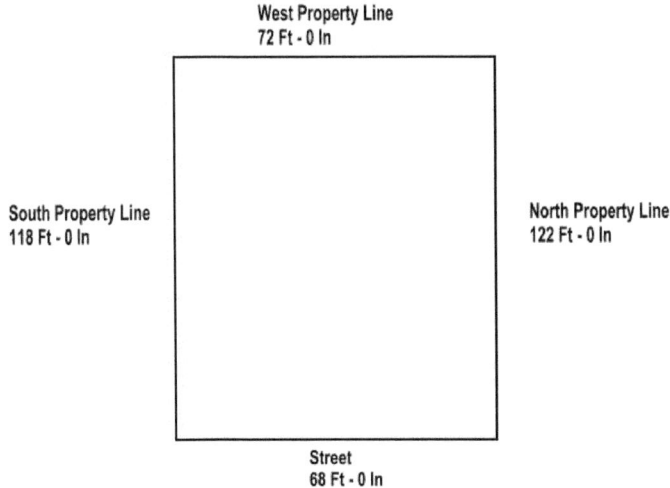

Step 3: To make sure the house is parallel to the property, or if the property lines are not parallel, site a reference line along one side of the house to locate the reference points "A" and "B".

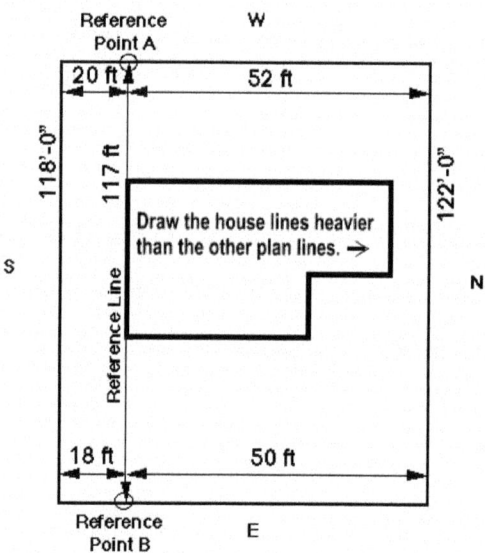

Step 4: Accuratley locate one corner of the house by measuring the distance from the back edge of the curb or edge of the street and nearest property line. From this corner of the house, measure each side of the house.

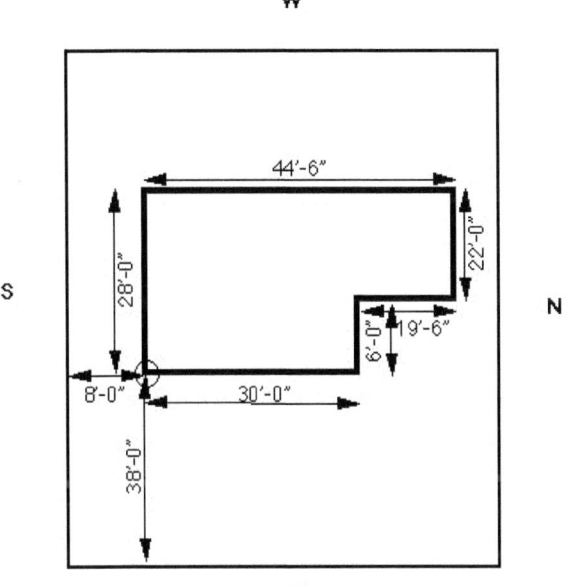

Step Five: Begin constructing a carefully drawn plot plan by selecting a scale to work with (1/8"= 1' or 1/4"=1') or by using graph paper. Begin by drawing the curb line as a double line or street edge as a single line. Construct property lines in the same manner as they were measured. Indicate compass directions.

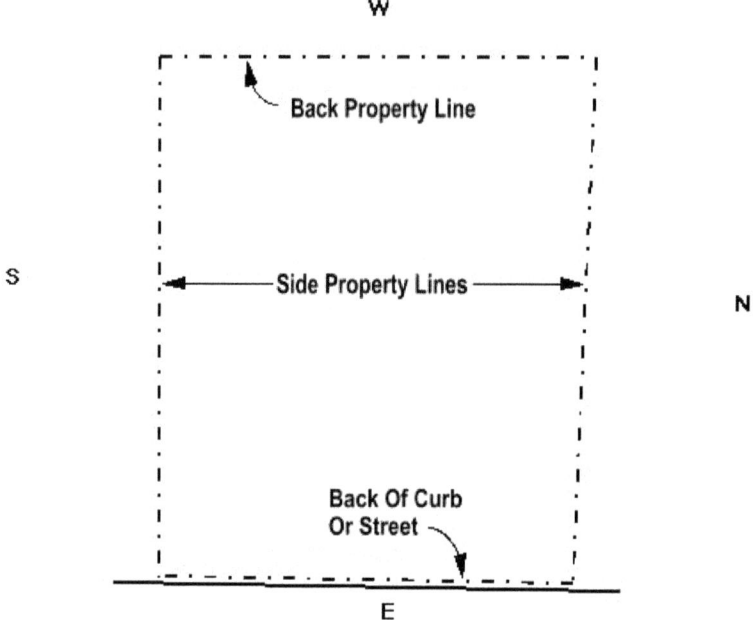

Step 6: First of all, note the city easement line, which is legally city property. The city may remove any planting or construction within this area for street widening, sewer work, etc. The exact location of this line will vary according to city ordinance. Next, locate one corner of the house using the two dimensions measured from the street and side property lines. From this point, extend a line representing the front of the house the same number of feet measured. Do the same for the

remaining sides of the house util you return to the original corner.

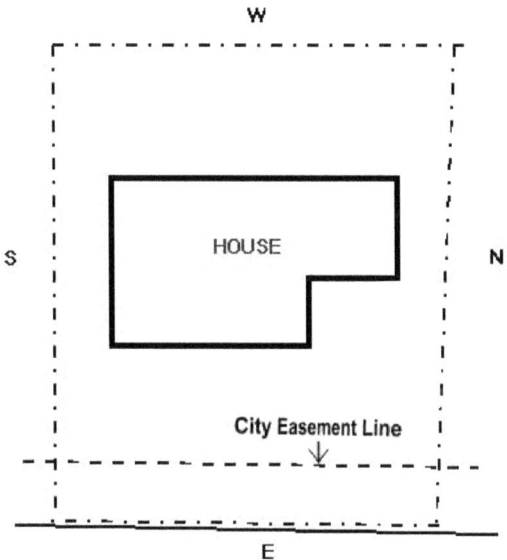

Step 7: Locate other existing features on a rough sketch by using the same method used for locating the corner of the house. By measuring from known reference points, such as the street, property line or house in two directions, the following permanent features can be located:

  A. Windows, doors and chimneys, including the height off the ground.

  B. All above and below ground utilities.

  C. Utility meters, electrical outlets and water spigots.

D. Natural or prominent features such as retaining walls, ravines and rock outcroppings.

E. Existing trees and shrubs.

F. Neighbor's buildings and landscape features near the property line.

G. Roof overhang on house.

All of these features should be measured and drawn on the rough sketch before drawing on the final plan.

Step 8: Transfer the information plotted on the rough sketch to the final plot plan. The plot plan is now ready to be used as the base for a home landscape design.

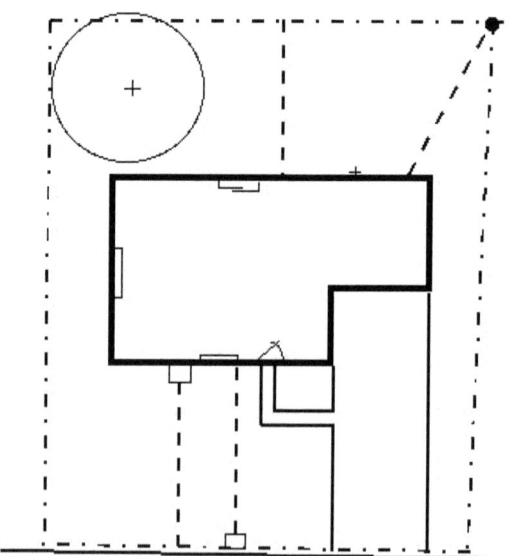

PLANNING FOR YOUR NEEDS

The next step in home landscaping is to plan for the needs of yourself and your family. List your needs. Consult each family member and consider there needs in your plans. These needs may include a driveway and turnaround space, off-street parking, play space for children, an outdoor living area, a vegetable garden, privacy from certain areas, windbreaks, etc. There are usually several ways of satisfying every need, and you must decide on the most appropriate one for you. The most satisfying landscapes are both *practical* and *beautiful*.

STUDYING THE SITE

Study your site. The piece of land you live on is generally referred to as the site. Ideally the selection of the site, placement and design of the house and the landscape development should all be done at the same time. Selecting a site without having some idea of the type of house and landscape development you want would be difficult.

Go back to the base plan you prepared in step one. Look closely at the problems and opportunities of your particular site. Tape a piece of tracing paper over the plot and prepare a rough sketch:

❏ Indicate major views from the inside looking out as well as the view on the site itself. Determine whether they are good or bad (for example: a direct view of the neighbor's trash or an open field of wildflowers).

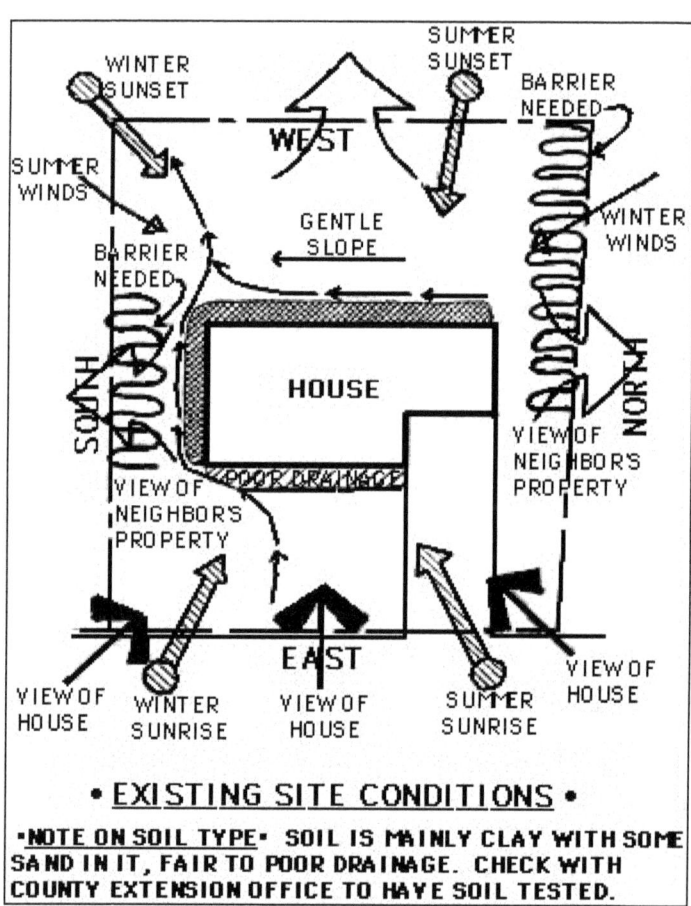

❑ Show exposure to summer breezes as well as winter winds. Also, indicate where you need shade.

❑ Indicate drainage patterns and slope of the land. Also, note any problems such as areas where water stands or needs to be redirected.

❑ Note the soil type and approximate depth, and have your soil tested. (For further information on soil testing procedures, contact your county Extension office.)

❑ Remove your tracing paper rough sketch and record this information as neatly as possible on your base plan.

Diagram

Diagram and place space needs. Again, tape tracing paper over your plot plan and go back to your list of needs from step two. Place needs and activities where they can serve best and provide enough space for each need. (For example: and outdoor living area should be of sufficient size for the use it will receive.) Rather than decide upon the shape of a lawn, terrace or parking area at the beginning, let these forms develop from and reflect the needs listed in the beginning.

The following areas are frequently found in the home landscape.

Develop each according to your family's needs and priorities.

Work or Service Area. The work or service area can be convenient, orderly and attractive. Lawnmowers, wheelbarrows, tools, insecticides and fertilizers all need to be stored in a dry convenient location. If tool and equipment space is not already provided, plan for one. Since many service areas are most convenient when adjacent to the garage or carport, consider adding your storage area to an existing wall. Garbage storage and clotheslines should be near the kitchen and laundry rooms. Allow at least four feet around the clotheslines to keep clothes from rubbing against fences, plants and walls. If only used occasionally, retractable or folding clotheslines may be the most practical. Service areas can also contain a compost pile or space for cutting flowers and vegetables. Consider screening the service area from view with either structures or plants to make it an attractive as well as functional part of the landscape.

Recreation or Active Sports Area. Features such as a swimming pool, shuffle board and tennis courts require considerable space and investment. A tennis court is normally

120 x 60 feet and a badminton court is 22 x 44 feet; swimming pools vary in size. If some of these facilities are on your list of needs but not practical for immediate installation, you may consider leaving open turf areas that can be used for badminton, other games and play.

Outdoor Living and Entertaining Areas. Terraces and patios are an integral part of many Texas homes and should be located, if possible, where they will receive summer breezes and afternoon shade. If sun is a problem, add trees of overhead shading structures.

Outdoor living areas are usually adjacent to living areas of the house where they can easily be served and seen from inside. With the cost of interior floor space at an all-time high, outdoor living areas can economically add entertaining and living space. Even when not in use, well-planned, attractive decks and terraces adjacent to the house give a feeling of added space to interior rooms. Attractive, long-lasting outdoor furniture and accessories (such as water features, sculpture and container plants) can be useful and enrich outdoor living areas. Some families have several outdoor living areas. Small terraces adjacent to bedrooms, bath areas and dining rooms are becoming more popular. A terrace may be placed away from the home to take advantage of a striking view. good breezes or the shade of an unusually beautiful tree.

Public and Entrance Areas. A large front yard is often a questionable use of land and resources. The parklike expanses found in some of our older subdivisions are pleasant but of little practical value. If your lot is small and building codes allow, consider developing the entrance area as a courtyard providing more use area for the family. If street parking is a problem use part of this area for off-street parking. Parking and enclosed front courts can be both attractive and functional.

Provide shade where it will most benefit your home's energy conservation. Keep plantings simple with shrub masses, groundcovers and flowering trees used to serve real purposes. Build walks and drives well and have them as direct and convenient as possible. Walks should be a minimum of 3 1/2 feet and preferably 4 feet wide. Provide a larger paved area at the entrance, if possible, since people tend to congregate there. A few container plants, small flowering trees or specimen shrubs help to make the home's entrance a focal point. Other features which focalize the entrance include architectural accessories such as attractive light fixtures, street numbers and front doors.

Children's Play Area. Locate the play area where someone inside the house can easily see it. A sand pile and swing sets are popular as well as paved areas for riding toys, play houses and tree houses. Keep the designs simple and easy to maintain and consider how the area might be used after the children are grown.

LANDSCAPING MATERIALS

Referring back to the diagram of space needs, begin finalizing the plan by refining the spaces into definite shapes. Now you are ready to choose materials. Try to choose materials that satisfy as many of your need as possible.

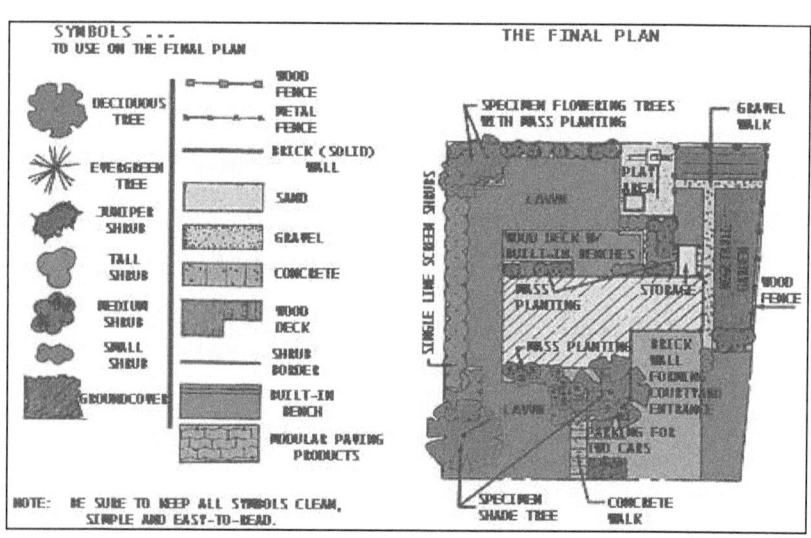

Sometimes non-living materials such as fences are a better choice than living materials such as a hedge. Both materials should provide privacy, but the hedge may require considerable time to grow where the fence provides immediate privacy. Also, if space is limited a fence may be the best solution. Maintenance is also frequently a concern. Usually non-living materials (brick, wood, etc.) require less maintenance than living materials which may require watering, trimming, etc.

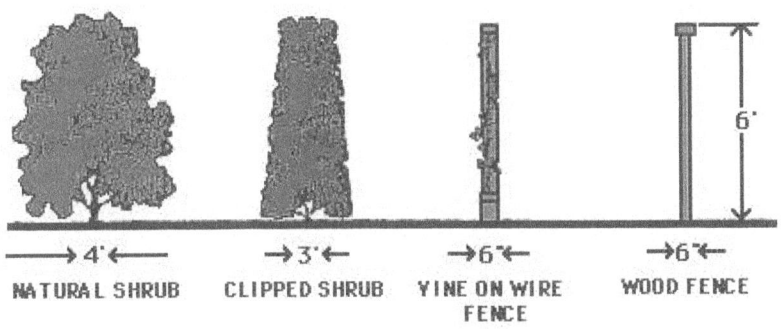

COMPARISON OF SPACE REQUIRED FOR SIX-FOOT VISUAL BARRIERS

One of the major objectives of good landscaping is to create a visual relationship between the house and the site. If your house is already constructed, you can still do a fine job of relating it to the site. Some of the ways this relationship between house and site may be achieved are:

- Use plants that are found growing naturally on or near the site.
- Repeat architectural lines of the house in the landscape - either with plants or construction such as walls, fences, etc.
- Use building materials that blend well in the natural environment or may be found there (for example: a wood shingle roof for a home on a wooded site or stone retaining walls in an area where the stone is found naturally).

Landscape design cannot be reduced to a series of rules. It may, however, be helpful for the homeowner to keep the following design concepts in mind as the design develops.

- *Group plants for emphasis.* Group the same plants rather than alternating shrubs or using many individual plants spotted about the property to provide a sense of unity and order.

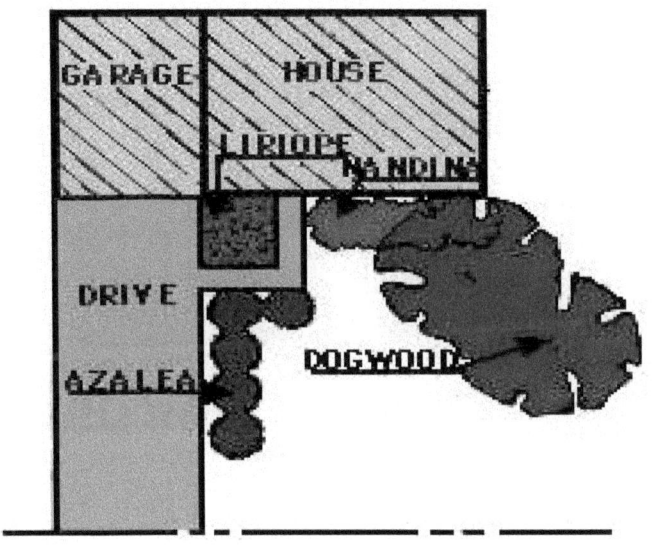

GROUP PLANTINGS FOR EMPHASIS

❑ *Plant trees for shade.* Trees of appropriate mature size should be used so that they will be neither too large nor too small for the house. Deciduous trees can usually be planted closer to the home than evergreens.

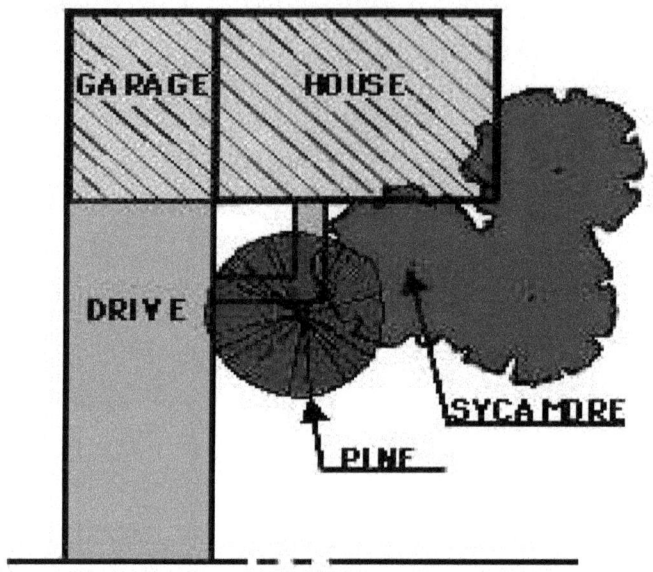

PLANT TREES FOR SHADE

❏ *Complement the structure.* Do not separate the house from its site by a ring of plants or foundation planting. Plants should compliment the lines of the structure, not set it apart from the site.

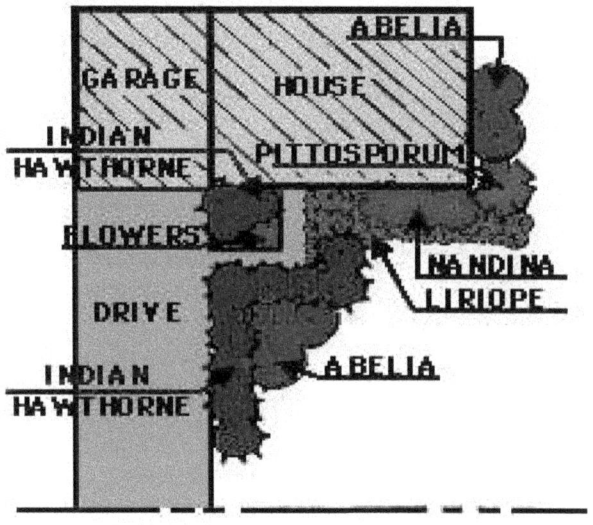

COMPLEMENT THE STRUCTURE

❑ *Provide privacy.* Instead of planting all the way around the property lines of your site, place screen plantings where they will provide privacy to exposed traffic and neighborhood activity. Use screening materials only where necessary.

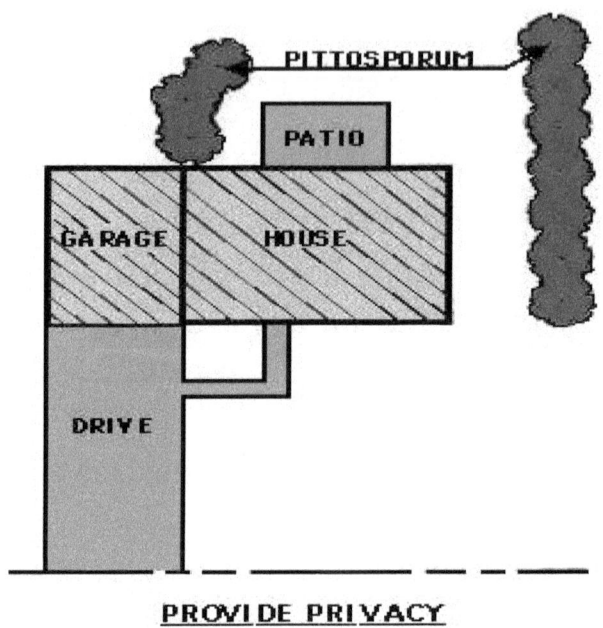

PROVIDE PRIVACY

❑ *Soften walks and drives.* Walks and drives in most cases serve only as aids in circulating people. When they are lined with hedges, border grass or other materials, they may become too prominent. Use enough materials to soften large areas of paving but allow the lawn grass to meet the pavements in most areas.

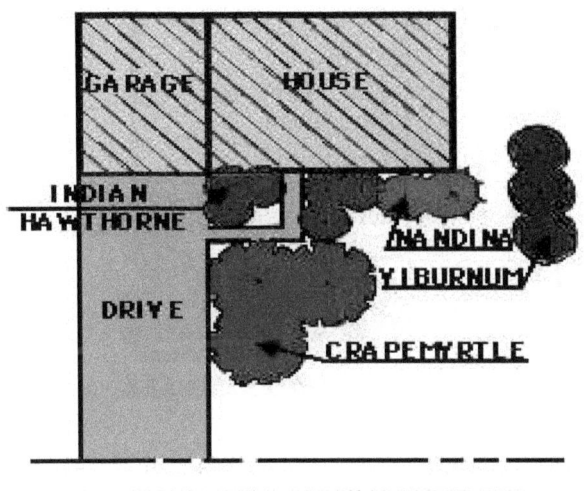

SOFTEN WALKS AND DRIVES

❏ *Allow space for ultimate growth.* Space shrubs in relation to buildings to allow for natural growth. Generally, no shrub should be placed closer than three feet from the building unless it is a groundcover or a plant which uses the wall for support. Do not be fooled by small plants in the nursery. Know the mature size of all plants you are using and space them accordingly. Plants should compliment, not cover a house. Select plants that require less maintenance.

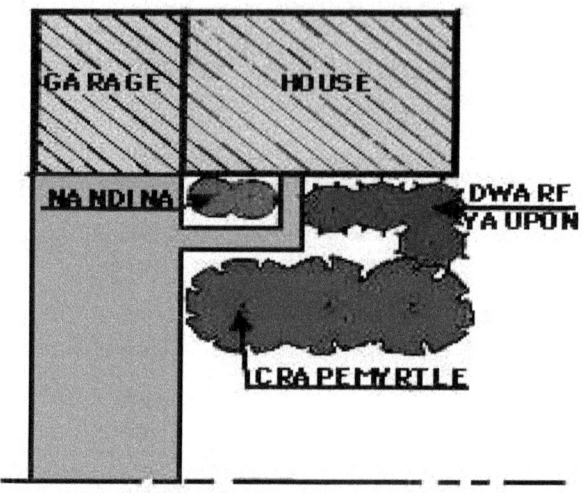

ALLOW SPACE FOR ULTIMATE GROWTH

❑ *Screen service areas.* Service areas should require small amounts of the site. Clothes lines, garbage containers, tool storage, etc. should be placed in a convenient area and screened from the living and viewing areas of the landscape.

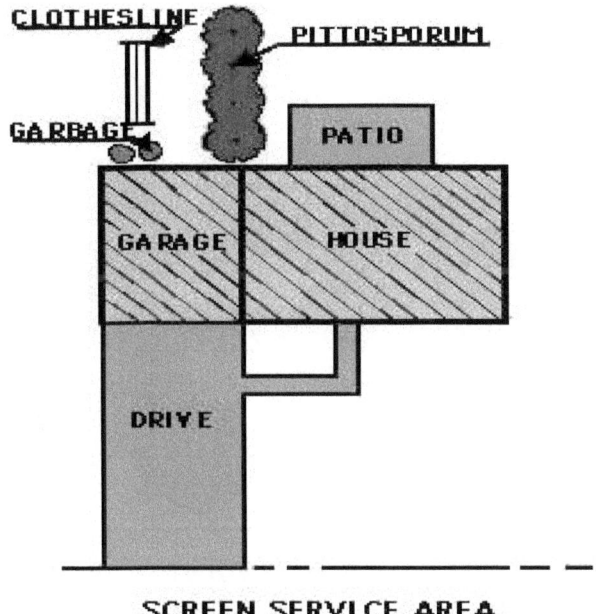

SCREEN SERVICE AREA

❑ *Use native plants.* They frequently withstand weather extremes and are usually more resistant to insects and diseases. Native plants can also be important relating a structure to its site.

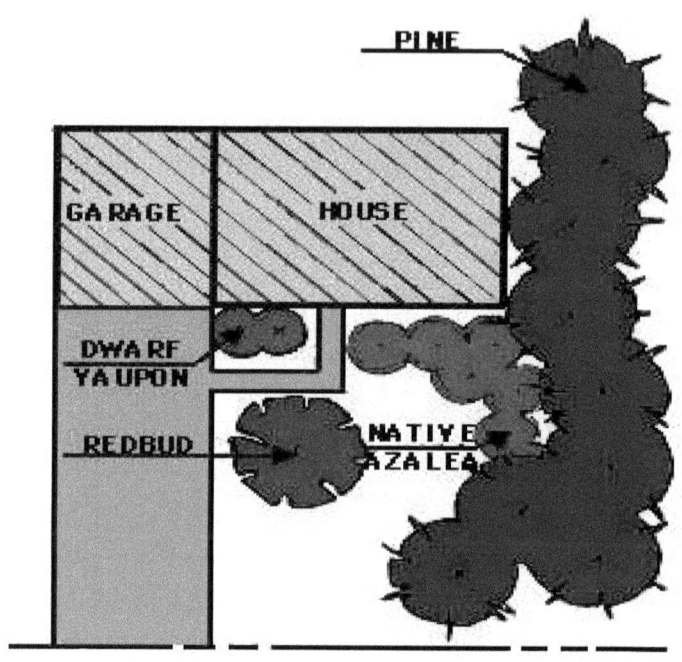

USE NATIVE PLANTS

PLACING YOUR PLANTS

Living trees, shrubs, vines, groundcovers, annuals and perennials are usually the most important materials in landscaping. Their selection, placement and maintenance are the main criteria the layman uses to evaluate landscape work. It is extremely important, therefore, to select plants that will serve the function as dependably as possible. For every landscape need there are numerous plants to choose from.

Plant Grouping. Plants are basically used as specimens, in lines, in groups or in masses. Each method creates a different effect.

Most landscapes will use all four types of groupings.

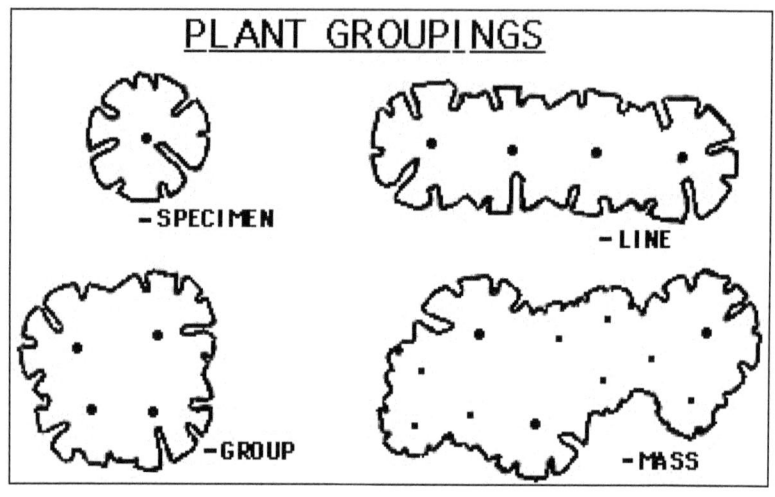

❑ *Specimen or accent:* You can use plants as specimens to emphasize a character shrub or an unusully interesting tree. Use sparingly an accent plant can can create interest and contrast. Flowering trees are commonly used for accents. Placing a specimen plant or small tree near the homes entrance can draw attention to that area.

❑ *Line*: Lines of trees, shrubs and other plants can help carry the home's architectural lines into the landscape. Straight or curved lines of tree plantings can shade parking or play areas or serve as a windbreak. Always select hardy, well-adapted plants to form a line since the visual effect can be spoiled if any of the plants become damaged. Also be sure that the same soil, drainage and sun conditions occur along the entire row since any of these factors will significantly affect the plant.

❏ *Group*: Grouping is a relatively natural way to use plants. Placing several trees, shrubs, etc. fairly close together will create a more massive effect. Since plants are often grouped naturally, this is a good method to relate your landscape to the natural environment.

❏ *Mass*: The mass is an extension of group planting. In mass plantings the individual plants tend to lose identity. Mass plantings are useful for relating larger buildings to the site since these plantings can be large enough to be in scale.

Selecting, Final Planning, and Purchasing

Landscape professionals can help you choose and locate new trees, shrubs, or ground cover. Share your drawings and tentative ideas with your local nursery or landscape contractor. As long as you have defined intended uses and spaces in which planting is actually possible, a competent nursery or landscape specialist will be able to help you make decisions.

When planting trees, shrubs, hedges, or bushes, find out how large the mature specimen will grow. In all cases, determine spacing by the mature sizes. For those plants close to your house, plan for at least 1 foot (30 centimeters) of extra clearance between the full-grown shrub and the wall of the home. This will prevent heavy pruning or damage to home siding in the future.

After considering the placement of your trees and consulting landscaping and nursery professionals, go back to your drawings or plans and add the new information on species, shape, and mature-size spacing. This provides a final, pre-purchase review to make sure that all elements will work well together - in the short and long term.

CHOOSING AND PLANTING YOUR PLANTS

Plant selection is often the key to good landscaping. A landscape will only look good if its plants are healthy and growing strong.

When choosing plants for the home landscape take into consideration their preferred site, level of maintenance, mature size, season of bloom, and susceptibility to pests.

Plan Ahead

Before purchasing any plant, study your site to determine whether you have mostly shade or sun, how wet or dry your yard is, and what soil type you have. These factors will help you decide which plants to choose for your landscape. Some plants prefer moist shade with acidic rich soil, while others prefer dry, hot, sunny areas with poor soil. By choosing plants that are well adapted to the conditions in your yard, your plants will thrive without much special care.

Time & Energy

It is also important to consider how much time and energy you want to spend caring for your plants. Roses are beautiful, but in general they require a lot of maintenance. They must be pruned, sprayed, watered, and dead-headed regularly to produce good results. Many people are more than willing to dedicate the time needed to maintain roses in order to get the gorgeous flowers, but others are not as enthusiastic about yard work. Look into how much care individual plants need before buying them.

What to Buy

Many plants are sold in garden centers and nurseries in 1 or 3 gallon pots. These plants are usually quite small and it is easy to forget that they will probably get much larger once planted in the ground. By carefully considering how large a mature plant will be before planting it, you can save yourself a lot of work, time, and money. Many people plant too many shrubs in a bed because they want the bed to look complete right after planting. However, they will have to come back later and remove whole plants or prune severely each year when the plants mature. Also, consider that there are often many different varieties of the same plant and each variety will have a different mature size. For example, there are hundreds of varieties of crape myrtles. Some are barely 1 ft. tall when mature, while others reach 40 ft. or more at maturity. If you have space for a 14 ft. crape myrtle, do some research to find a variety that will only be 14 ft. at maturity.

Perpetual Motion

The best landscapes have something interesting going on at all times of the year. They may have pansies blooming in the spring, perennial wildflowers blooming through the summer, a sugar maple with beautiful red and orange leaves in the fall, and hollies which keep their showy red berries through the winter. Choose plants for your own landscape that will give you interesting colors or textures throughout the year.

Hardiness Zones

USDA Plant Hardiness zones are often used to determine if a plant will grow well in an area. Hardiness zones are based on the average cold temperatures for an area. Therefore, areas of the country with similar average low temperatures will all be in the same hardiness zone.

Because USDA Plant Hardiness zones are based on the average cold temperatures of an area, there is no guarantee that a plant listed as growing in zone 7 will actually thrive in a specific location within zone 7. Various parts of the same zone can vary in the amount of rainfall they receive, the average high temperature, the soil type, and many other environmental conditions. However, the USDA Plant Hardiness zones can give us a good idea of how a plant will perform in our area.

Irrigation

Everyone enjoys the site of colorful crape myrtles in bloom and the delicious flavors of fresh vegetables in the summertime.

However, to keep garden plants at their best throughout the summer, they will need to be watered regularly. While watering your plants may seem simple enough, there are some tricks to watering the garden that may help your plants grow even stronger.

Most plantings around the home, including lawns, flower beds, and vegetable gardens need 1 to 1.5 inches of water or rain each week during the growing season. If there is a good soaking rain during the week, you can probably avoid watering. Otherwise, you will need to irrigate. It is best to water deeply and infrequently.

You should avoid watering more than twice a week because frequent, shallow watering encourages shallow rooting. Your plants will be stronger and better able to tolerate stress if they are well-rooted.

You can determine the amount of water supplied by your irrigation system by placing a shallow container, such as a coffee can or glass jar, in the area being watered. Make a mark on the container one inch from the bottom. Then, time how long it takes for the water to reach the 1 inch mark on the container. If you live on a slope or have compacted soil, water may run off before it has time to penetrate the soil. To avoid run-off, reduce the volume of water you are putting out so that it takes longer to fill the container to the 1 inch mark. If you can't control the volume of water, you can water for a short time, wait a few minutes to allow the water to soak in, and then water again.

The best time of day to water your plants is in the early morning. Watering in the morning conserves water by allowing it to soak into the ground without evaporating. Avoid watering at night because foliage will stay wet all night long leading to disease problems. Watering during the middle of the day also has its problems. Each water droplet that sits on a plant's leaves will act like a magnifying glass and burn the leaves of your plants in the sun. In addition, if overhead irrigation is used during the middle of the day, much of the water evaporates before it ever reaches the ground. Watering in the morning conserves water, allows greater penetration of water, and reduces disease problems.

A good, thick layer of mulch in gardens and around trees and shrubs can greatly reduce the amount of water required by plants. Mulch reduces evaporation from the soil and cools the soil. In addition, mulch can act as a barrier to weeds which compete with your garden plants for water. Many different organic materials can be used as mulch including tree bark, chipped wood, pine needles, grass clippings, or dried leaves.

While water is essential for plant growth, it is possible to overwater. Plant roots need air as well as water and are not able to get enough air when flooded. We often see landscape plants die during the summer months due to overwatering rather than underwatering. Use the container method to determine how much water you are applying and don't apply more than 2 inches of water per week. There should never be standing water in a flower bed or garden.

Plants will flourish during the summer months if cared for properly. Watering correctly is one of the best ways to keep your plants looking great all summer long.

Trees

Trees provide us with many things - from lumber for houses and furniture, to food from apples and pecans. While we may have a few fruit trees in our yard, the main reason we plant trees in our yards is for beauty or shade.

Shade trees that are properly located on your property can cut summer utility bills by 20 percent or more. For energy efficiency it is best to plant deciduous trees on the west side of your house.

Trees planted in these locations provide shade during the intense heat of the day. If you use deciduous trees, they=ll lose their leaves in the winter, allowing the sunlight in to help warm things up during the coldest times of the year. It will also help if you shade your air conditioner. This can increase the cooling efficiency by as much as 10%.

Think about heat in the summer. Even large scale parking lots are opting for tree planting. And everyone fights to get the spot in the shade. Research has proven that there is a significant temperature change on paved surfaces from planting a tree.

There are numerous species of trees that make great shade trees, from many of the oaks, (including willow oak, shumard oak, cherrybark oak and pin oak), to tulip poplars, bald cypress, and even sweetgum. There is a new sweetgum on the market that doesn=t produce sweet gum balls, called >Rotundifolia=.

Not only are these large trees giving us shade but they are also helping to clean the air. Leaves on trees absorb carbon dioxide, and filter pollutants from the air. They also catch airborne dust and dirt, and give off oxygen. Not only do they work on air pollution, but also noise pollution. They absorb sound, and can create a buffer between you and a busy street.

Tree roots are often blamed for many problems, but rarely thanked for controlling erosion. The canopy of the tree shelters soil moisture and helps in erosion, but so do the trees roots. Trees planted along a riverbank can slow the water and reduce flooding. If you live in an area with high winds, a diverse planting of trees can act as a windbreak if properly planted.

Think of the beauty of trees, from the massive trees fall foliage to smaller trees flowers. Dogwoods have been the most popular blooming tree in Arkansas for years, but others are coming to the forefront now. For more sunlight look at the Kousa dogwood.

There are sweetbay magnolias, golden raintree, chinese fringe tree and redbud. Japanese maples are popular under story trees and flowering cherries and crabapples are a nice addition to springtime color.

Select a tree for your landscape based on what you need. Do you need and have room for a large shade tree? Do you want a small under story tree for color? Before you plant a tree, look up. Make sure power lines are not going to interfere with growth. Try to locate trees no closer than 15 feet from the foundation of your house. Check the drainage.

Trees come in three ways: balled in burlap, bare root or containerized. They also come in many sizes. Choose one that you can easily manage. For larger and more instant shade, there are now professionals with giant tree spades that can move large trees. Container grown plants can be planted any time you want to. Balled in burlap trees should be planted before the heat of summer sets in or again in the fall. Bare root trees need to be planted when they are totally dormant since there is nothing inside the plastic sleeve to sustain plant growth.

When you plant your tree, be sure to plant it at the level it is currently growing or slightly more shallow. Work up the planting hole wider than necessary to encourage the roots to spread out. Avoid amending the soil in just the planting hole, or you encourage the roots to stay in the planting hole. Avoid fertilization at planting, but do water well. Mulch around the tree to keep grass and weeds away which can compete with the young root system. And continue to water once a week all season to help the tree get established.

Tree Planting

Fall is for planting. Often heard, but more often overlooked. Planting hardy trees and shrubs in the fall of the year can allow the plants to form a good root system before they have to contend with the heat and humidity of our summers. If you had to pick the best time to plant a tree, fall and early winter is it!

November is ideal. As the leaves begin to fall, and the trees go dormant, plant away.

Plants usually come in one of three forms-container grown, balled in burlap or bare root. Today, more and more plants are being grown in containers, and container plants can be planted twelve months out of the year-provided they are given some care. Yes, even in the midst of a horrid July, you can plant trees and shrubs, but plan to stand next to them with the garden hose. Balled in burlap and bare root plants should be planted while they are dormant. Regardless of what form they come in, planting in the dormant season, (which is beginning) puts less stress on the newly planted plants. There is usually ample natural moisture, which allows the new plants to begin forming roots without much care from us. Do pay attention to the weather and if we go without natural rainfall for several weeks, you will need to water, even when it is cold.

Choose your plants wisely. When planting trees, look up. Don't plant under or near power lines. Give the tree ample room to form its natural shape and canopy. Today, many power lines and cables are being put underground. Know where these lines run before you begin digging. Consider the width of a mature tree as well.

Normally we don't want to plant a shade tree any closer than fifteen feet from the foundation of the building.

Choose plants that take the conditions you have. If you have a moist boggy soil, go with plants that like moisture. Likewise don't put something that likes water, such as a River

Birch in a dry, rocky site. Working within the parameters you have, make life a lot easier on you and the tree.

There are many misconceptions about planting trees or the way a trees root system grows. Some people claim that the trees root system, mirrors their top growth. Not true. Most plants have the majority of their root system in the top six to twelve inches of the soil-even trees. The entire root systems of most trees can be found within three feet of soil. The spread of the root system however, can be very extensive, often extending 2-3 times the spread of the crown. When planting a new tree, digging holes to China isn't helping anyone-except perhaps the chiropractor. If possible, dig a hole a minimum of three times as wide as the plants root ball, but only as deep as the root ball is. Don't replace the existing soil. Many gardeners throw away the rocky, poor soil, and backfill with potting soil or other rich amendment. That is not going to help the plant at all. Instead, it will containerize the plant in the ground, or create a swimming pool-either situation is not good for you tree. You can amend the fill by mixing organic matter with the existing soil. By amending a wide area and digging a wide berth, the root system will be encouraged to spread into the surrounding soil. If all you do is amend a hole large enough to plant in, you containerize the plant in the ground. Where would you rather grow, in the nice rich potting soil in the hole or the pitiful rocky clay surrounding it? If you can't amend a wide area, don't amend at all. Make sure the depth of the hole is only as deep as the root ball, or slightly shallower. You need to allow for some natural settling of the soil, and you don't want to bury the plant too deep. The majority of the roots on the newly planted tree will develop in the top 12 inches of soil. If the tree is planted too deep, new roots will have difficulty developing due to a lack of oxygen. No fertilization should be used at planting. You want the root system to settle in and begin to grow the first season. Top growth can be more of an issue in year two.

Once the tree is planted, apply mulch around the tree to a depth of two to four inches. Allow some space between the mulch and the stem of the tree. You don't want those volcano mulch beds often seen around town. I often refer to them as the "bed and breakfasts" for rodents. Mice or voles can live in the nice moist, warm mulch bed, and reach over and chew on the trunk of the tree all winter long. Leaving that air pocket keeps moisture away from the trunk of the tree.

Mulch is important because it moderates soil moisture and temperature, it looks more attractive and keeps weeds away, and it keeps plant competition away. Lawns do compete with the roots of trees for water and nutrients, and if the lawn was there first, it can out compete those new tree roots. Mulching in a wide berth, also can prevent lawnmower and weedeater disease- the damage often done to the base of trees.

Once planted water is the most important factor for success. Too much or too little can both lead to death. Make sure the site is well drained and water deeply to encourage root formation.

If the tree is structurally sound, staking should not be necessary. Studies have shown that trees will get established faster and have a more stable trunk if they are not staked. However, if you have a tall or large tree with a fairly small root system, or live in an area with high winds, or have trees that have suffered storm damage, occasionally staking is needed. If staking is needed, use two or three stakes used with a flexible tie material. You want to allow some natural movement, so don't stake too tightly. Any ties that are in contact with the tree should be flexible, or wrapped in a piece of hose tubing. You don't want to cut or wound the trunk of your tree with the support. Remove any staking and ties after the first year of growth.

Trees provide us with shade-a much cherished commodity in the summer. With proper planting, they will establish themselves quickly, and begin a long and prosperous life. If you need new trees in your landscape, now is a wonderful time to plant.

Perrenials Bulbs

Dig a hole, drop in a bulb, then sit back and wait for spring. For the lazy gardener, or those in a hurry, spring bulbs provide us spectacular spring color, for very little effort in the fall. And now is the time to plant them.

When you mention bulbs, most people immediately think of daffodils and tulips. And while they are wonderful bulbs, there are many other bulbs to choose from. Some different small flowers include snowdrops, crocus, grape hyacinths, winter aconite, and anemones. Larger flowers include Dutch iris, flowering onions called alliums, fritillaria and the crown imperial fritillaria. Of course don't exclude daffodils, hyacinths and tulips.

What Are Bulbs?

Bulbs are self-sufficient storage organs, and are versatile in the landscape. There are bulbs for partial shade as well as full sun. All bulbous plants have similar life cycles. They go through periods of growth and flowering, followed by a dormancy period. Some are spring growers, while others grow in the summer or fall. Bulbs are usually sold in their dormant, dry state. When planted, they being to initiate rooms, and the stems inside the bulbs begin to grow.

The plants utilize their stored food reserves, and the shoots begin to emerge. When they begin flowering, the storage organ or bulb, is empty of food. After bloom, they need to replenish the storage organ for the upcoming dormancy.

Choosing Bulbs

When choosing bulbs (or rhizomes, corms, and tubers, which we collectively call bulbs, and are generally planted in the same manner), look for large bulbs, which are firm and blemish free.

The size of the bulb determines the size of the flower. Remember, everything is already contained inside your bulb when you purchase them. Quality bulbs will give you a wonderful show, and should keep giving for years with a little care. Bargain bulbs may not end up being such a bargain.

Choosing a Site

Be sure to choose a site with well drained soil. Even bulbs which like moisture, won't survive for long in water logged soil. Bulbs thrive in an environment rich in organic matter, and a porous soil. Incorporate organic matter before planting, and till it in well.

Generally, bulbs need to be planted two to two and ½ times the size of the bulb, deep in the ground. Bulbs can be planted individually using a bulb planter. They also sell an auger drill bit that will fit on the end of your drill to make the planting holes. But if you are planting a large quantity of bulbs, it is easier and quicker to dig up a large area to the required depth, then space out the bulbs and cover them with soil. Be sure to plant the bulbs with the pointy end up, and use care when covering the bulbs with soil, that you don't knock the bulbs over in the process. When you have the soil in place, water well and mulch to keep weeds down. Since the bulbs are underground, you can also plant seasonal annuals, such as pansies or snapdragons on top of the bulbs. In the spring, the bulbs will emerge within your annual color.

Fertilization

Fertilization is really not necessary at planting, but many people add bone meal around the bulbs to aid in root establishment.

Fertilization is needed during the growing season to aid in the replenishment of the bulb. Fertilize once when the flower buds are beginning to open with a slow release fertilizer, or a general purpose fertilizer can be used when they show color, and again when the flowers have faded.

Bloom Life

To extend the length of blooms, do a little homework. With proper variety selection you can have color from late January through April, all with spring bulbs. Decide where you need color, and what else is growing there, and when it blooms. You wouldn't want to plant hot pink tulips next to orange blooming azaleas, if they are in bloom at the same time. Color selection is important. Although your personal preferences are of the utmost importance, knowing which colors work together can help in the final outcome.

Colors

An easy division of color is the cool versus warm colors. Reds, yellows and oranges are warm colors, while blues, purple and pinks are cool colors. Warm colors are intense and invigorating, while cool colors are peaceful and harmonious. Make sure your color choices blend in well with your existing landscape and home. The most successful plantings use solid blocks of color. Keep your color schemes simple, and only use a few colors.

Types

The earliest bulbs include winter aconite and crocus. These small growing plants are rich in color, and can be planted in dappled shade to full sun. Crocus bulbs come in a variety of shades of white, yellows and purples. Crocus bulbs can be planted in your lawn area, simply removing some plugs of grass, then plant the small bulbs. The plants will emerge in the lawn area and by the time you need to mow for the first time, they will already be through. Winter aconite or eranthis, is not as common, but has lovely yellow, honey-scented flowers.

Snowdrops or galanthus, and snowflakes or leucojum are old- fashioned flowers. These small bulbs do best in partial shade, and have pretty white flowers. Bluebells and scillas are other good choices for a woodland bulb planting. They flower in mid spring and have lovely hyacinth like clusters of flowers in shades of blue, purple, pink or white. Grape hyacinth are lovely small flowering plants with dense spikes of purple flowers. Many have attractive spiky foliage which appears in the fall. When you talk about small flowers, remember that you will need more plants for a big impact.

If you are an iris fan, there are bulbous iris that bloom in early spring, and the foliage dies down at the end of their season.

Dutch iris make a beautiful show in the spring, and you don't have to deal with the foliage year-round.

Some other unusual flowers are the flowering onion or flowering alliums. Height will vary by variety with dwarfs no taller than six inches to the giant alliums that can grow four to six feet tall. All of the alliums produce round flower heads, and come in shades of pink, purple or white. These unusual flowers can really add a focal point to your garden.

The fritillarias offer another interesting flower for the garden. This member of the lily family blooms in late spring, and bears its flowers in a cluster at the top of leafy stems. The impressive crown fritillaria is a show stopper in late season.

Experiment with new and interesting bulbs, but don't forget the tried-and-true. Hundreds of varieties of daffodils, tulips and hyacinths are available. Tulips, which provide one of the showiest displays, is often hard to get to bloom well again. This year, many of the local nurseries are offering heritage bulbs, or the old- fashioned tulips. These are supposed to rebloom better for us - we'll have to wait and see. Regardless of their rebloom, no garden would be complete without some tulips. And if it is scent you are after, hyacinths are a must. And the spring sentinal for many is still the daffodil. Besides the traditional yellow, there are pinks, doubles, whites, and oranges available.

Bulbs are excellent for spring color, whether used as a mass planting, or in a mixture with other perennial or spring blooming shrubs, or in containers. The choices of colors, heights and bloom periods offers so many opportunities. Visit your local nursery and look at the options, then plant. Bulb planting season is from now through December.

Ferns

When we think of ferns we think of moist wooded settings. And while there are many ferns for the shades from moist areas, to drier hillsides, there are even ferns that will grow in full sun.

There are ferns that can grow on rocks, in sand, or totally submerged in water. All types can be found commercially, but you may have to search for them. In the past ten years, hardy ferns have become much more available.

There is a nationwide resurgence of growing hardy ferns, and the commercial suppliers are trying to meet this need, using advanced propagation procedures with tissue culture production. Instead of growing hundreds of plants for sale, they can now grow millions of plants. The supply is now getting into all arenas of sale.

Shade Ferns

Shade ferns for the garden are a diverse mix, including hundreds of species. Some good starter small ferns include: Maidenhair fern: Adiantum pedatum –this fern has fronds which hang down like locks of a damsels tresses, thereby its name. It has a bluish green foliage, and will add delicate texture to your garden.

Another small fern which is also evergreen, and is the most hardy native fern, both in shade and drought tolerance, is the Christmas fern: Polystichum acrostichoides. This fern has a more upright growth. It is named Christmas fern because its green foliage was gathered and brought indoors during the holidays and made into wreaths and garlands during the Civil War era, up through the early 1920's. Sensitive fern: Onoclea sensibilis is another interesting low growing fern. This fern changes its form when disturbed by early frosts or by hot weather in spring. This leads to various leaf forms. In the fall, this fern is one of the first to lose its leaves. It also prefers a moist environment.

Shield Ferns

Moving up the scale, (three to six feet in height) are the shield ferns: Thelypteris spp. Shield ferns will generally tolerate more drought and have a more lacy appearance to the leaf. Shield ferns are what define our definition of a fern leaf or frond. There are more than 100 varieties of shield ferns in the commercial trade, ranging in height from two feet to four feet.

The leaf color is generally a lighter green to hunter green, and tend to grow in a vase shape of fronds. Log ferns: Dryopteris spp. tend to be larger–up to six feet in height, and a darker green in color. They have a fuller, coarser leaf, with less cutting in the fronds. There are several hundred varieties in the commercial trade, and six native species.

Cinnamon and Royal Ferns

Cinnamon and royal ferns: Osmunda spp. are common throughout Arkansas and were one of the first ferns that homeowners began finding in garden centers. Royal ferns can grow up to six feet in height, and generate many fronds. In time they form dense colonies of plants, giving a bushlike appearance in the landscape. They will die back completely to the ground in the winter. The cinnamon ferns new fronds emerge covered in a reddish hair, and are called fiddleheads. This is not the edible fiddlehead of commerce don't eat the Arkansas natives. As the fronds age, the red hairs drop off, but a few are retained where the little leaflets join the main stem of the leaf. The spore bearing leaves come up first and are quite red in color. The sterile persistent green leaves follow, and are also covered with reddish hairs initially. The spore bearing fronds only last a few weeks, and will wither away, leaving behind the large green bushy leaves.

Sun-Loving Ferns

If you are a fern lover, but don't have shade, don't despair. There are sun-loving ferns. It is even possible to grow some of the shade lovers in the sun, but soil preparation and water are crucial to survival. An easy family of ferns to grow is the Lady ferns: Athyrium spp. There are two native species and several hundred cultivars in the trade. They differ by the amount of cutting in the leaves, with colors ranging from reds to greens. Some cultivars are dwarves–no taller than a foot, with other varieties growing upwards of six feet. The southern lady fern is supremely adapted to a wide range of sun and soil characters. They can be quite drought tolerant, after they are established. These plants will grow in both full sun to total shade, but will require more water, and a more organic soil in the sun.

Bracken Fern

Another sun lover. Give it space, for it is aggressive. It will tolerate the shade, but prefers the sun–growing three to four feet in height. It tends to kill out other plant species in its shade, so give it its own space, and let it grow–and more importantly give it room to grow.

Care

As with any group of plants, culture and care will vary by species. Some general guidelines for all ferns: prepare the soil carefully.

Loosen the soil and add in well-aged compost or leaf mold. Avoid tight, heavy soils. Have your soil tested, if the pH is below 5.5 add some pelletized lime. Most ferns prefer a soil pH between 6.0 -7.0. Raised beds make for excellent fern displays but will need extra winter protection – with mulching. Raised beds have lower winter soil temperatures which can be harder on the ferns. Container gardening of these ferns can be difficult both in summer temperatures and winter lows. Wrapping of the pots or using larger containers may help. Container production of hardy ferns should be limited to some of the smaller ferns, which don't produce as large of a rhizome and root system.

While many of the ferns can be drought tolerant once established, most ferns will benefit from supplemental watering. Ferns appreciate an occasional leaf mold or aged compost supplement, but don't respond well to commercial fertilizer. For the most part, if proper soil preparation was done, they should do fine on their own.

Ferns prefer to be left alone to multiply – they like benign neglect– and don't like to be divided on a regular basis. So allow room for them to mature and spread. Division is a method of propagation, but will set back their growth for a year or more.

Ornamental Grass

When we think of grass, we typically think of the type we mow, that covers the majority or our yard, or the type that we weed from our flower and vegetable beds. But a whole family of ornamental grasses exists that have a place in the landscape.

There are low growing spreading forms, to large clumps with graceful blades. They are at home in any landscape, and are an easy and carefree addition.

Most grasses are at their peak in the fall, with an array of colorful seed heads. Grasses offer a diversity of color, form and texture to the landscape year-round, but really add interest for fall and winter. Grasses can even add sound to the garden in rustling foliage and dried seed heads. Most grasses perform best in full sun, although there are some shade lovers in the bunch. Given the variety of mature sizes, it is best to investigate the plant, before selecting one. Learn the eventual height and spread, to ensure you get exactly the type of grass you are looking for.

When we talk about ornamental grasses, we aren't limiting ourselves to strictly members of the grass or graminaea family. We're also including grasslike plants, including sedges, rushes and even some members of the lily family.

Choices

Growing grasses as ornamentals isn't new, but the variety of choices is. Many of us are familiar with, and have been growing, the giant pampas grass for years. And using grasses for fresh and dried flower arrangements, have been popular since Victorian times. These days there is a desire to have low maintenance landscapes, and naturalistic landscapes are becoming quite popular. We also are trying to branch out of spring only landscapes, and have interest for every season, so the search is on for additions to the fall and winter landscape. Enter grasses.

Divisions

Grasses can be divided into two major divisions - those that clump, and those that run. Unless you are looking for erosion control, or need the ground covered quickly, you may want to avoid the runners. Running grasses spread by means of underground stems known as rhizomes, or above ground horizontal stems known as stolons. They can be invasive, and hard to keep contained. Clump formers are less competitive, but again, depending on variety, they can take up room in the garden over time. They blend in better in the typical landscape.

Size

Next consider size. There are upright, vertical forms, arching plumes or low mounding forms. There are giant forms reaching 12 feet or more which can be used as accent plants or screens, or wispy delicate forms for ground covers. And not all grasses are green - and remember there are various shades of the color green itself. Some grasses are blue, varietated white or yellow, and some have outstanding red, purple or even black foliage. And consider their dormant season color in shades of tan, as well as the color of the seed heads. One type, the Leatherleaf sedge is light brown year round.

Maintenance

Ornamental grasses are relatively low-maintenance. There are few pest problems, and most are fairly drought tolerant, although a few flourish in wet environments. They usually benefit from a shearing at appropriate times of the year - for most grasses this is before growth begins in the spring.

Perennial & Annual Grasses

While most of us are adding grasses to the landscape that are perennials, there are also some annual members of the family to look to for color and interest. These include the small cloud grass, Agrostis nebulosa, Big Quaking Grass, Briza maxima; Job's tears, Coix lacryma-jobi; Rabbit's tail grass, Lagurus ovatus; and my favorite the Purple Fountain Grass, Pennisetum setaceum 'Cupreum'.

If you are looking for small grasses in the landscape consider bulbous oat grass, a white and green variegated plant growing 12 to 18 inches in heigh. Side oats grama, is a 2 foot tall plant with an arching growth habit, that is very drought tolerant. And if moist soil is a problem, consider one of the ornamental sedges (no, not nutsedge). Leatherleaf sedge has coppery brown foliage year-round and is a great border plant. Japanese sedge has some interesting plant variegation and makes an attractive arching mound. Another neat plant is the dwarf blue fescue, Festuca ovina 'Glauca'. It forms dense tufts of blueish green plants, that makes an interesting ground cover or low border to the garden. Bearskin feskue looks like a little green porcupine in the garden, with golden spikes forming in the center.

Annuals Pansies

As the leaves begin falling, and our flowers start to fade away, many gardeners put their gardens to bed for the winter months. The idea of months without flowers seems a waste, especially when we can have an outstanding display of color from pansies all winter long. So instead of ending your gardening for the year, begin your winter gardening with a planting of pansies.

Pansies, come in a variety of sizes, colors and types. They come in blues, reds, yellows, white, orange, pink and purple. There is even a black variety. There are solid colors without faces, to bi- colors with contrasting faces, to blended colors, giving you a mix of colors in each bloom. Intense breeding has developed flowers that can get as large as four and a half inches across, on lovely green foliage. It is hard to believe that these large, brightly colored flowers are descendants of the quiet, diminutive woodland violets.

Flowers

The flowers have a velvety texture and bloom over a long period of time. They also last quite well as a small nosegay or bouquet indoors. To keep the plants blooming, be sure to deadhead - remove spent flowers as they decline. Pansies thrive in cool weather, and will bloom for you from now until hot weather causes them to decline next summer. Plant them in a well-drained location with moderately rich soil. They will grow in full sun to partial shade. Those in full sun will fade away sooner in the summer, but by then you have plenty of other plants to replace them with.

Varieties and Colors

When it comes to varieties of pansies the list continues to grow each year. Some of the most common classes of pansies include Majestic Giants, which are one of the largest classes of flowers, and the first pansy to be awarded an AAS - All American Selection. Almost all varieties in this series have the traditional dark blotch or face, and they come in blue, purple, white, yellow and red. The Crystal Bowl series of pansies are bright flowers which are clear colors (without faces or blotches). The flowers are smaller, but there are lots of them - these plants are very floriferous. Colors range from white to yellow, true blue, rose, orange, violet and a scarlet color. The Crown series of pansies are also clear colors with slightly larger flowers ranging in color from orange, red, white, yellow and blue.

Some unique types of pansies include the Imperial Antiques which give soft, blended colors. Each flower changes subtly from opening to maturity. Another interesting series is the Joker series. One interesting combination is Jolly Joker F2 Hybrid, it combines an intense orange lower petals with a deep purple (almost brown) upper petals. The Joker Light Blue has an outstanding flower with a light purple outer color with a white band leading to a dark purple blotch. The list could go on and on, with new intense shades and mixtures each year. Go visit your local nursery and see what is available that you like.

Pansies can be planted in a mix of colors, or for a really dazzling display, in a single color. Plant the individual plants four to six inches apart. Mass them together wherever possible. They make a great companion planting for spring flowering bulbs. Simply dig up the bed, plant the bulbs first, cover them with soil, then plant the pansies on top. The spring bulbs will come up right through the pansy plantings for even more color in the spring.

Container Plantings

Pansies also make ideal container plantings. If you live in an apartment or condominium, don't think that you are excluded from planting pansies. Plant a container full for your deck, patio or front porch. Regular watering will need to be included in their care - even when it is cold. It is especially important prior to a heavy freeze. They don't need to be saturated, but they do need to be moist.

Fertilizer Requirements

Fertilize pansies regularly all season long. Fertilize at planting and during any warm spell throughout the winter. They respond well to blood meal, but several gardeners have also attracted wild animals to their pansy plantings by using it. If you want to use blood meal, incorporate it into the soil lightly. Be careful not to be too heavy handed, since it is a high nitrogen fertilizer. Any commercial fertilizer will work well also.

Bulbs

There are many who want to have a beautiful garden with little effort. While the old adage: ' if it sounds too good to be true, it probably is', usually applies; in the case of bulbs, we get a break. You can simply dig a hole, plant a bulb and sit back and wait for the flowers to come. It is the story of the ugly duckling turning into a swan. In a manner of months, these small, nondescript brown things turn into glorious displays of flowers, with minimal effort, and in many cases, they will continue to flower, year after year.

By definition, a true bulb is a modified leaf bud, consisting of a basal plate, short thick stem and fleshy scales. It contains all plant parts and serves as a storage organ. But for now, lets just lump all underground storage organs as bulbs. This will include the corms, rhizomes, tubers and pips. If you plant it in a dried, bulbous state, and wait for the leaves and flowers to appear, we can give it the name "bulb". Do consider that when you buy your bulbs, everything is already contained inside it-the flowers, the leaves and the stems. Therefore, the larger the bulb, the larger the flower will be, and it should bloom its first season in the ground. Whether or not it blooms the next year will be determined by the care it gets while it is growing. Once its seasonal cycle is complete, everything is once again set for the following season.

There are two main classes of bulbs-spring blooming and summer blooming. Summer bulbs are still growing in our gardens and are preparing for their dormant season, while spring bulbs are just being planted. Some of our bulbs are hardy and can stay in the ground year-round, while others do need to be lifted and stored for the winter.

Summer bulbs which can stay in the garden include cannas, lilies, Liatris, elephant ears, peonies, crocosmia, and lycoris (the surprise lilies and Naked Ladies). Summer bulbs with marginal hardiness include gladiolus, dahlias, calla lilies and tuberose. Non- hardy bulbs which should be lifted and stored for the winter if you plan to keep them include caladiums, achimenes, and many of the amaryllis. To store the bulbs, lift before or immediately after a killing frost, let them air dry for a few days. Cut the old foliage off, shake off excess soil, and place in a cool dry place in a cardboard box, onion sack, etc. -

not plastic. Replant in the spring after all chances of frost have passed.

For hardy spring bulbs, planting season is upon us. While the more common bulbs include daffodils, tulips, crocus and hyacinths, there are more options. Within the individual bulb groups there are options-sometimes too many to choose from. With careful selection you can start with snowdrops and crocus in January and end with flowering onions in June.

When planting bulbs, grouping them together in clusters will have a stronger impact than a single row of bulbs. Grouping them by season of bloom and color will also help. A mass planting will make a huge impact in the spring, and they can easily be planted under your winter annual plantings of pansies, violas and kale.

The bulbs will come up around them and add to the seasonal color display. Unless you are growing the bulbs as annuals, and replanting each season, consider the foliage needs after blooming. All spring blooming bulbs require a minimum period of growth following bloom, which should last at least six to eight weeks.

While bone meal is the staple fertilizer at planting-(and remember when we plant we cannot alter flower size, we are simply aiding in root establishment,) bulbs do like a more complete fertilizer during the growing season. They aren't picky and it isn't hard to do. Simply scatter some complete nutrition - 13-13-13 or whatever you have on hand will work fine, around the bulbs when the foliage is well established but before they begin to bloom. You can also use a light application as soon as they finish flowering.

Allow the foliage to grow healthy for at least six weeks following bloom. While some gardeners do allow the foliage to begin yellowing before removal, that can often take months-in a good growing year. That isn't necessary, but it also won't hurt. Do avoid braiding or twisting the foliage-that can hinder food manufacture and means you need a hobby!

When planting your bulbs, you can dig individual holes for each bulb, but that can be a lot of work in our rocky soils. It is often easier to dig up an area, scatter your bulbs in, and then fill the soil back in. A general rule of planting is to plant two to three times the size of the bulb, deep in the ground. Small bulbs are planted shallow, while big bulbs need a deeper hole. Choose a site with good drainage-especially in the winter. Standing water and bulbs is not a good combination.

Spring bulbs are out there in abundance now. While you can always add to your collection of daffodils or hyacinths, consider some of the more unusual bulbs. Even within the old tried and true daffodils, there are some unusual options. Not all daffodils are yellow, some are white, some have orange or pink centers, some are fragrant and some aren't. By careful consideration you can have daffodils in bloom from late January through April. Most daffodils are long lived, and provided they get some sunlight following bloom, will re-bloom year after year.

Tulips aren't quite as easy. Tulips are usually one of the last of our spring blooming bulbs to flower. Warm temperatures during bloom can cause the flower display to pass quickly, and often the leaves are quick to follow. This coupled with the fact that many of the new tulips produce many daughter bulbs, making them share the energy, flowers in subsequent years are often smaller. Many gardeners treat tulips as annuals, planting new ones every year. If you don't want annual planting, consider some of the species tulips or earlier bloomers.

There has also been a resurgence of the heirloom bulbs which tend to take more abuse than some of their showier new siblings. Regardless of which flower you choose, or how long they last, tulips are definitely the showiest spring bloomer, and worth the effort.

Crocus bulbs may not stop traffic because of their demure stature, but they are the harbinger of spring, and a reliable performer year after year-sometimes even too vigorous. Give crocus room to spread, because they will multiply. Crocus bulbs are often interplanted in lawn areas. They grow so early and are low enough growing, that they can give your lawn an early blush of flowers and their cycle is complete by the time you need to do the first mowing.

Hyacinths are one of the most fragrant spring bloomers with clusters of pink, purple or white flowers. They also will rebloom with ease for many years, but do require annual fertilization.

Old-fashioned snowdrops and snowflakes will give you beautiful bell shaped white flowers in early spring, and will do well in a more shady location. Wind anemones will pop up early in the fall with lacy foliage, and bright colorful flowers. They aren't going to be around for too many years but are an interesting addition.

Others to consider are the showy and large Crown Fritillaria with its crown of orange flowers, or the showy giant alliums, large lollipop-like flowers with a delicate onion fragrance.

Experiment with bulbs, and you may find some new favorites. Fall planting is easy-the hard part is the wait

Vines

If you need some fast solutions for some simple problems, look to vines. Whether you need a living screen, or you want to cover a trellis or arbor, or you need some temporary shade, or you simply want to add some color to a stark wall, annual vines have much to offer. They are among the most rewarding plants in the garden, giving you a wonderful display in one season, and taking up little room in the garden. And unlike their perennial or evergreen counterparts, they won't need pruning, and they won't become invasive.

Vines add a vertical dimension to make small spaces seem larger, and they provide privacy and cooling shade. Most annual vines won't cling to a brick or wooden wall, like their more permanent counterparts, but you can use such climbing aids such as wire fences or trellises to support them.

Many of our annual vines are actually old-fashioned plants. Most old home sites used vines which clambered up the side of the house, or clothed a trellis in foliage and flowers, or turned a sunny porch into a cool, leafy retreat. Why not choose these carefree plants to soften your landscape. They are easy to grow, use a minimum amount of ground space, and are pest free all season long.

Annual vines are easy to grow in flower beds, hanging baskets, window boxes or trellised planters. They transform unattractive areas, and provide a quick and inexpensive solution to many landscape problems. By using annual vines you can vary the plants you are using and your color scheme every year.

While some annual vines will reseed themselves every year, for others you have may want to save your own seeds or buy new plants. Most of them are heat lovers and will not kick in and grow until the soil and air temperature warms up. Even though they may be slow to get started, they thrive all summer long, right up until frost. And since they are "annuals" they only last one season.

There are numerous annual vines to consider. Many nurseries now offer not only the seed, but small plants as well. Check your local garden center or nursery to see what is available. Cypress vine and cardinal vine are closely related members of the morning glory family. They both have outstanding crimson flowers which are attractive to hummingbirds. The cypress vine is Ipomoea quamoclit and has very delicate fern like foliage. It can grow ten feet or more in height and has delicate star shaped blossoms. It does best in full sun to partial shade. Cardinal vine, Ipomoea x multifida has a slightly larger, more funnel shaped flower, almost like a miniature morning glory but in bright red, it has a wider leaf blade than the cypress vine. It will also grow at least 10 feet tall. It does best in full sun.

Don't overlook the common morning glory, Ipomoea purpurea. While it may be a weed in some fields, there are numerous varieties and colors to choose from, and they have extremely showy flowers. Colors include the true blues, pinks, whites, lavenders and magenta, as well as two tone flowers. They have large heart shaped foliage and the flower size can vary from as small as two inches up to 5 inches. Full sun to partial shade is best, with this vigorous vine. Some varieties may reseed freely, so learn to recognize it. It is considered one of the most reliable bloomers, unless the soil it too rich.

Another member of the morning glory family that has become a popular vine is the moonflower, Ipomoea alba. Unlike other morning glories which open early in the day and are often closed by evenings, moonflowers don't begin their show until evening. As if to emulate the summer moon, these six inch white flowers open every evening at sunset. Not only are they beautiful flowers, but they are fragrant to boot. If you can find a plant, buy it. They can still be started from seed now, but it takes at least twelve weeks or more for the plants to begin blooming. Full sun to partial shade.

And don't forget the ornamental sweet potato vines, which are also in the morning glory family, Ipomoea batatas. While they are a true sweet potato, they are grown for their attractive foliage rather than their production ability. While they can produce a tuberous root that is edible, it is not highly rated, and rarely eaten. From the dark purple 'Blackie' variety to the chartreuse leafed variety 'Margarete' and a newer variegated foliage plant called 'Tricolor', these vines rarely, if ever flower, but they produce copious amounts of leaves which can spread up to 12 feet or more. These ornamental types were discovered in the Philippines in the early 1980's.

And lest you think all annual vines are morning glories, there are some other highly prized plants. Hyacinth bean is an old-fashioned vine, making a big comeback. Hyacinth bean, Dolichos lablab, is a fast growing member of the pea family with large purplish tinted leaves with dark purple stems. If this weren't attractive enough, by mid-summer it is covered in deep lavender pea-like flowers.

These long lasting blooms, are then transformed into glossy purple four inch seedpods, which are every bit as pretty as the blooms. It will grow up to 15 feet in a season. Uncooked beans and flowers are poisonous. Full sun to partial shade.

Two other members of the bean family are the runner beans: scarlet runner and Jack and the Beanstalk. The Scarlet runner bean, Phaseolus coccineus produces large vines with attractive scarlet flowers that also attract hummingbirds. You can eat the flowers, pods and seeds of this versatile bean. Jack and the Beanstalk, Phaseolus multiflorus is another edible runner bean. This prolific vine can grow 20 feet or more and has beautiful white flowers followed by edible beans.

If you want to have a utilitarian vine, you can also grow gourds. From luffa's to the bottle gourds, many of these make large vines with showy yellow or white flowers, followed by the hanging gourds themselves.

Another old-fashioned annual vine is the black-eyed Susan vine or clock vine, Thunbergia alata. Flowers may be orange, yellow or white, with or without a black center or "eye". The common name clock vine comes from the fact that the vine will twist around its support in a clockwise motion. These vines can be grown in a hanging basket, or it can climb a trellis, six to eight feet in a season. Partial shade is best, and this is not a drought tolerant plant, so be prepared to water.

Hops, Humulus lupulus, is another fast growing vine that is legendary for its inclusion in beer brewing. It is grown more often for its ability to quickly cover a trellis or arbor and provide summer shade. It has sand paper like leaves and aggressive tendrils that twine at will. A herbaceous plant, it dies to the ground in the winter, and may return in late spring to sprint upward its 15 to 30 feet summertime growth. After it dies back, getting it off an intricate structure can be tricky, so keep it your staking or trellising simple. By the way, it is the flowers that are used in beer. Actually it is the bracts and while both male and female Hops make flowers, only the ripened cones of the females are used to brew.

There are other annuals vines on the market. Asarina, commonly called creeping gloxinia, is a member of the snapdragon family.

This vine is native to Mexico where it reaches great heights. It should grow at least ten feet tall, and blooms best in the sun. Flower color varies from shades of pink to purple. Cobaea scandens, or the Cup and Saucer Vine produces interesting flowers that start out as green papery buds and open to reveal the green saucer and bell-shaped flowers. They start off white, changing to deep purple before falling off. This sun-lover can grow twenty feet or more.

There are a few newer plant introductions that are actually tropical plants, that can serve as summer annuals. Mandevilla, the fast growing pink flowering vine, blooms its heart out all summer long with flowers ranging in shades of white to light pink to a dark hot pink. Allemande is a yellow flowered vining plant. There are also several clereodendron's that will spread some and give you outstanding color all summer long.

Whatever the intended use or location, there's an annual vine to suit your situation. For most, it is plant them now, then stand back and let them grow.

SHRUBS

Native Shrubs

Go native! More and more gardeners are opting for plants that grow naturally in our state, or for that matter, were around before we were. Naturalistic gardens, or taking some pointers from Mother Nature, is on the upswing. What better way to have a natural garden than by using plants found in nature.

Why this sudden craze for native plants? One reason, is that if they've survived so well on their own, think about how well they'll do in your own garden given a little TLC. They have to be durable if they have survived the vagaries of our climate without weekly watering and frost protection. Often, natives have adapted defense mechanisms to pests common in their areas, or they have a high tolerance for pest damage. Therefore, natives tend to be more maintenance free than some of our exotics. But, what are natives, and how do you find them?

Common Natives

Some of the plants you have grown for years are native plants and you just didn't know it. Things like Carolina Allspice (Calycanthus floridus) is native from Virginia to Florida, Yaupon holly (Ilex vomitoria) is native as is the American holly and the Savannah holly. Redbuds and dogwoods, and oakleaf hydrangeas all have their roots here. Natives aren't just unruly weeds.

While some purists believe that you should uproot all non-natives or exotics, there is room for both. If you have an existing landscape, try adding to it some native plants - from perennials to trees. If you are starting from scratch, you may want to incorporate more, simply to cut back on the maintenance.

Native Vines

While we aren't going to list every native plant available, here are some that should be locally available and would be good to start out with. For vines there is the trumpet creeper - Campsis radicans, with bright orange to red flowers in full sun. It does best where it has poorer soil, tending to grow vegetatively in rich soil. A kissing cousin is Cross vine, Bignonia capreolata, with dark red tubular flowers which are yellow throated. It grows statewide.

Then look at the honeysuckles. We don't want the invasive Japanese honeysuckle, Lonicera japonica - which isn't native anyway; but there are some wonderful trumpet honeysuckles from Lonicera sempervirens, which comes in shades of red and orange and a rare yellow. Then there is the standard Virginia creeper, a plant commonly mistaken for poison ivy,. Virginia creeper grows well in shade to partial sun and has one of the prettiest fall colors of any vine other than poison ivy, which most of us don't want. For shadier gardens, you can plant a harder to find vine in the climbing magnolia-Schisandra glabra, or there is the climbing hydrangea, Hydrangea anomala, a deciduous vine with flat white flower clusters, and a wonderful peeling cinnamon bark.

Native Shrubs

Some interesting shrubs for the landscape include the French Mulberry or Beautyberry - Callicarpa americana. While the plant is not anything to shout about during the early growing season, it produces outstanding clusters of purple or white berries which encircle the stems from late summer through fall, giving you great color when you really need it. Another old fashioned deciduous native is the Carolina allspice, or sweet shrub - Calycanthus floridus. This shade loving plant grows rapidly and produces flowers at an early age in late spring. The common plant has a reddish brown colored flower with a wonderful spicy aroma, but there is a rare yellow form with an almost citrusy scent available at Ridgecrest nursery. The variety is Athens. Another wonderful shade native is the Euonymus americana, commonly called strawberry bush or wahoo. This plant has tiny yellowish green flowers in the spring, but outstanding strawberry red fruit in the fall which pop open to expose bright red seeds. These can persist well into fall.

An interesting family to experiment with is the witch hazel family. Hamamelis vernalis, the vernal witchhazel and Hamamelis virginiana, the common witchhazel are both native shrubs. Both have very fragrant, spiky yellow flowers, the vernal one in January - March, while the common plant blooms in the fall - seasons when we need interest and color. Their fall foliage is also outstanding. Another member of this family is the fothergilla.

Fothergilla gardenii produces white puffballs of honey scented flowers in April to May, and it too has great fall color. These plants do best in full sun to partial shade and prefer an acid pH.

Hydrangeas

All of us are familiar with hydrangeas, and there are some native plants. One favorite is the Oakleaf hydrangea, Hydrangea quercifolia. These are great plants for the shade/ woodland garden. They produce lovely panicles of white flowers in early to mid summer, which persist all summer. Then the fall foliage is spectacular. As they age the bark peels and gives them an interesting winter habit as well. Give them room to grow as they can grow six feet or taller and spread wide. Another native hydrangea, is Hydrangea arborescens. This is a native lacecap hydrangea. Some improved cultivars which should be readily available are 'Annabelle' and 'Grandiflora'.

Hollies

Hollies are a popular addition to landscapes, and some of them are native plants. One of the most common hollies - the Yaupon holly is native as is the Savannah and American hollies. One often overlooked member of this family is the deciduous holly - Ilex decidua and Ilex verticillata. Commonly called possum haw or winterberry, these plants have a profusion of berries in the winter, which really stand out once the leaves are shed. Some outstanding selections include 'Council Fire', 'Warren's Red', 'Sunset' and 'Winter Red'.

Virginia Sweetspires

Virginia Sweetspire, Itea virginica is an easy and outstanding plant to grow. It produces white fragrant flowers in May each year. It is very adaptable doing well in full sun to heavy shade, tolerates a wide range of pH and soil conditions - from moist to dry. It also has outstanding fall foliage.

Illicium's

Another group of native shrubs is the Illicium's or Anise plants. Illicium floridanum comes in white or red flowered varieties. The Illicium parviflorum is a hardier performer and produces a larger mass planting. Makes a good screening or hedge plant in a shady, moist area in your yard. The Florida anise plants look better in more shade. If exposed to much sunlight, they tend to be a thinner plant.

A Favorite (Azaleas)

The number one landscape plant tends to be the azalea. But there are native azaleas that can be a wonderful addition to your landscape. You can get colors and scents unheard of in evergreen hybrids, and they are much more tolerant of our weather conditions - both summer and winter. The only downside for some people, is that they aren't evergreen. These shrubs can grow quite large in time, and typically bloom in mid to late spring. One of the most fragrant of these is Rhododendron alabamense, the Alabama azalea. It produces white flowers, blotched in yellow and can grow up to eight feet in height. Rhododendron arborescens or the Sweet Azalea produces white to pink azaleas with red styles, grows five to six feet in height. The Flame azaleas, Rhododendron calendulaceum produces some wonderful yellow and orange varieties. So instead of opting for all evergreens, plant some of these or other wonderful deciduous varieties. They will pay you back with graceful blooms every spring without the fuss of the evergreen type.

Viburnums

There are also some nice selections of viburnums which are native. Most people are familiar with the snowball bush - (which is a viburnum, just not native). Some native members of the family include Arrowwood viburnum, Viburnum dentatum. Indians used the stalks of this plant to make arrows, since the wood was strong and straight. It will form a large shrub with white flowers in late spring to early summer. Viburnum nudum is another early summer white bloomer, with rapid growth. Following flowering clusters of berries form which change colors over time. 'Count Pulaski' is an introduced plant from Ridgecrest Nursery. Viburnum prunifolium, the Blackhaw viburnum will grow quite large, forming a small tree or large shrub. Similar in appearance to a hawthorne tree, it has small white flower heads in May, followed by a berry.

Taller Natives

As you can see, you have more options than you knew when it comes to native shrubs. If you need taller plants - those we could call tall bushes or small trees, you could also plant the fabulous native Grancy Greybeard, Old Man's Beard or White Fringe Tree - Chionanthus virginicus. It's clusters of white fringe like flowers in the spring last longer and, to many, beat a dogwood, hand down. They also require a lot less care. There are also numerous magnolias for the landscape. While many think only about the large-growing Southern Magnolia, there are some great native varieties with a smaller size. These include Sweetbay magnolia, Magnolia virginiana, the Bigleaf Magnolia - Magnolia macrophylla, and if you want something almost tropical in appearance, plant the Umbrella Magnolia, Magnolia tripetela. It has the appearance of a giant scheffelera in your garden, and it's hardy.

Woody Natives

While this is not the only native woody plants that we can grow, it is a good start. Some will be easier to find than others, but check with your local nursery to see what they have. There are also a few nurseries in the state that specialize in native plants. While I don't recommend digging up every non-native plant in your yard, to plant all native plants - add a few natives and see how you like them. NEVER, go searching these plants in the wild to plant in your yard. If everyone did that, there would be none left for the rest of us. Unless you own the property, you don't have the right to dig anything up. Its also healthier on the plant, and easier for you to purchase them from a reputable nursery.

If your yard needs some local flavor, or some interesting new plants that can almost take care of themselves - plant native shrubs.

Antique Roses

What goes around, comes around, is an old, but true statement. If you look at the cost of what our mothers considered "junk" or the clothes today that looked like what I wore in junior high, you'll find the craze for the past is up and going. Antiques aren't just for furniture and clothing, they are also big in the plant world.

Heirloom plants are finding a niche market and filling it. Everything from vegetables to flower varieties are being brought back to our gardens. And roses are high on the list of antique flowers.

Beloved for centuries for their wonderful scents, and their unique and beautiful flowers, rose lovers everywhere are adding antique roses to their gardens, in the hope of having their cake and eating it too - or in other words, having roses without weekly spray programs. For while all antique varieties aren't immune to the dreaded black spot disease, most of them don't get it or suffer little from its effects. But why did they go by the wayside, and are just now returning, if they are so wonderful? Several things can be considered. First, hybrid tea roses came on the market and offered much larger blooms in many cases, and almost constant bloom throughout the growing season. Their flowers were more defined and lasted longer. So we went with the new plants to get bigger and more flowers. We traded scent in many cases, and ease of growing. We now spray weekly, prune severely yearly and are much more tied to our gardens than before. Who today has time to devote to weekly pesticide sprays? And, many having the time, choose not to spray.

What is an old or antique rose?

The American Rose Society classifies an "old" rose as any rose introduced before 1867. Many gardeners consider it old if it has survived 75 years or more. Many of the antique roses are pastels, you won't find many bold colors. They almost all have good fragrance, and often have a season of bloom - not all season.

There are some who have a repeating bloom period. They don't need the drastic yearly pruning, tending to be shrub or climbing in nature. This too makes them easier to handle. There has been a great deal of research on old roses, and you can find many books on the subject as well as entire nurseries devoted to propagating and selling old roses. So they aren't nearly as hard to come by as they used to be. While there is still an active "rose rustler" group out there, who scours old cemeteries, home sites and abandoned fields, in search of new "old" varieties, we have a good collection of plants that will do well in our gardens. Antique roses by growth habit lend themselves to blending in with existing landscapes, or creating wonderful archways or flowing lines in our gardens. We don't have to devote entire beds to roses because of their special needs, they can be mainstreamed into our gardens. A few naysayers, have asked why they would want a rose bush that only blooms four to six weeks? Yet their gardens are comprised completely of azaleas, a plant we're lucky to get four to six weeks of bloom.

Classes or families of roses

Antique roses are divided into classes or families of roses. These include: Chinas, Noisettes, Polyanthas, Musks, Old Europeans, Bourbons and Teas

Unique Characteristics

Each division has unique characteristics, but still offers a wide variety of color and bloom. If you are new to the antiques, visit your local nurseries and see what is available. Visit the local rose growing societies, and visit with gardeners who have them. Then experiment. Some possible starters include:

'Mermaid' which is a vigorous and thorny plant. It blooms from late spring until frost with large, single yellow flowers. It grows quickly, blooms long, but does have big thorns.

"Old Blush" is a common old rose, with again, a long blooming period. It blooms profusely with double light pink blossoms in the spring, then slows down a little during the hot dry summer, and bounces back in the fall. This vigorous shrub rose gets five to six feet in height and spread.

`Zephirine Drouhin' is a wonderful climber with thornless stems. It is extremely fragrant with semi double dark pink flowers primarily in the spring, with a smaller show occasionally in the fall. The growth habit, coupled with thornless stems makes this one a winner.

`Cecile Brunner' is an all-time favorite. Both bush and climber varieties are available in this durable and long blooming plant. The flowers begin as a pink bud and open to a cluster of light pink flowers. The profusion of blooms in the spring is followed all summer by a few blooms all summer and again a show in the fall. Highly disease resistant, it can't be beat. The climber is tougher and a better plant I think than the bush form.

`The Fairy' has been available and popular for a long time. This sprawling bush gives off hundreds of sprays of tiny double rose pink flowers, which fade with heat, giving you a white bloom. It begins blooming in late May but will continue to bloom provided it has ample moisture.

'China Doll' is a small border or edging rose, growing no taller than eighteen inches. It begins blooming late in the spring and continues through fall, with clusters of pink blooms. It has a nice compact growth habit and has good disease resistance.

'New Dawn' has pale pink flowers which bloom heavily in the spring, scattered blossoms in the summer with another show in the fall. It is a wide growing rambler rose, and bears the distinction of being U.S. Plant Patent No. 1, the first rose patented under federal regulations. It has been touted as good hedge material.

These are just the tip of the iceberg. There are hundreds of old roses out there. While most roses perform best in full sun, there are some antiques that tolerate light shade. Good drainage is important, and preparing your soil prior to planting can insure success, as with any other planting. Find out the eventual size of your roses when you plant them. If they have the potential to spread fifteen feet, allow for it. Give them time to grow and fill in. Allow a little air space around them for better air circulation to help with diseases. If you have a fence or need a living arbor, plant climbers that can spread, but give them their support from the beginning.

Care of Antique Roses

Antique roses are not as demanding as the hybrid teas for fertilizer and water - many will do well with little fertilizer and once established, may be drought tolerant, but especially with the ever bloomers or repeat bloomer, you will have more flowers if you pay attention to watering and fertilize occasionally.

Diseases and insects usually don't plague these plants much, but as with any plants in your yard, nothing is resistant to everything. Monitor them occasionally for problems, and catch them early.

They will not require the weekly sprays of other roses. For pruning, you need to know the growth habit of the plant and its season of bloom. For spring only bloomer, treat them like azaleas, and prune after bloom. For ever bloomers, shape as needed before growth begins.

Finding Antique Roses

Read the catalogs or information that comes with the plant to see what to expect. If you find an old rose in your yard, do nothing the first season, to see when it blooms naturally.

Antique roses are grown on their own root system-they aren't grafted. They root easily and with care, can be rooted almost any month of the year. Keep the cuttings moist and make sure there are no flowers, buds or hips attached to insure quicker rooting. Use a rooting hormone to speed things up. This is an easy way to find new plants, find friends who are willing to share. If you can't find friends, ask your nurseryman what he has and what they can get.

If you gave up on growing roses, because black spot wiped you out year after year, think again. The antique roses can give you graceful forms, interesting textures and color, with an added bonus of fragrance, and for the most part, you don't have to spray.

Hibiscus

Hardy or hearty, tropical or perennial, wildflower or cultivated plant, whichever hibiscus plant you have, they are a welcome spot of color in our gardens and homes. These members of the mallow family, give you show-stopping blossoms, provided you have sunlight and give them the proper care.

The hibiscus genus includes a wide range of flowering plants. Hibiscus flowers grow in many forms. Their petals may be flared, cut or fringed, single flowers or doubles, and colors can run the gamut, from whites to reds, yellows to orange. Size of blossoms vary with species, as do plant height and leaf size and shape.

Some are deciduous shrubs, others form woody stalks, but die completely to the ground each winter, and others are tender, and must be brought indoors for the winter. Some bloom non-stop, even indoors provided with the right care, others bloom most of the summer, and still others only bloom in the fall. Hibiscus plants are in the same family as okra and cotton - two heat lovers. As such, hibiscus plants typically don't get started growing until the air and soil temperatures have heated up, so be patient in the spring and wait for your perennial forms to sprout. Knowing which plant you have, will determine how you take care of it.

Tropical Hibiscus

The tropical hibiscus or Chinese hibiscus (Hibiscus rosa-sinensis), has the most prized and showy flowers, but it isn't winter hardy, so must be moved indoors for winter protection, or new plants purchased each year. These have become a popular addition to our gardens each summer, and have become readily available statewide. Flowers range in color from pinks, to reds, yellows to orange, with single flowers or doubles available, all with shiny, evergreen leaves. Plants range in size from small 4 inch pots to standards or even braided topiary specimens. This plant has been widely cultivated, and there are hundreds of cultivars world-wide. They make excellent container plants or nice annual color in a hot, sunny spot in your garden. Each flower usually only lasts a day, sometimes two, but a healthy plant should have constant bloom.

They prefer a well drained soil, and frequent application of fertilizer in the summer to keep blooming well. Flower buds may drop if the plant is moved to a different climatic area–such as indoors to out, or vice versa. They may also drop buds if the soil gets too dry. Whiteflies can be a problem. If you do choose to overwinter your hibiscus plants indoors, give them a cool, sunny room, and allow them to stay on the dry side. Prune them back one third to one half in late January or early February, to keep them full and bushy.

Perennial Hibiscus

The perennial Hibiscus moscheutos – our common rose mallow or marsh mallow can be found statewide in swampy areas. Large white flowers are the norm, on this tall growing plant. Numerous cultivars have been released as ornamental perennials, giving us the 'Disco Belle' series of two to three foot tall plants, to the larger 'Southern Belle' with six foot plus stalks. These plants bloom from June through early fall, with flowers as large as dinner plates. Colors range from white, to pink to maroon, with some bi- colors thrown in. While the plants do form large woody stalks, they die completely to the ground during the winter. They don't begin to grow in the spring, until the soil temperature has warmed up. Give them room to grow, since they can be quite large, over time. The more sunlight the better, and they do much better in a moist environment with high organic matter. The large, coarse leaves often are chewed on by various leaf eating insects. Unless it really takes away from the beauty of the plant, it doesn't hurt the flowering ability at all. Woody seed capsules appear after bloom. They can be planted in the spring, but often benefit from soaking overnight before being sown. You can also scatter seeds out in the fall, and allow them to come up in the spring.

Texas Star

Another perennial hibiscus, is the red blooming Texas Star or Hibiscus coccineus. Deep red, funnel shaped flowers are borne on this tall growing plant. Growing six to eight feet tall or higher, this plant can be identified by its lobed leaves. It also performs best in full sun, and in moist conditions, but can tolerate drier sites in partial shade. Crosses between this species and other perennial species have resulted in the 'Lady Baltimore' and 'Lord Baltimore' species which have pink flowers with red centers and vibrant red flowers respectively on four to five foot tall plants.

Confederate Rose

The last perennial hibiscus that is not as commonly grown, but worth growing, is the Confederate Rose or Hibiscus mutabilis. It has the potential for being the largest of the perennial hibiscus, growing 15 feet or more in one season. While not 100% winter hardy except for in the southern part of the state, this hibiscus has powderpuff-like blossoms, which open either white or pale pink and turn a darker shade late in the day. It blooms in the fall only, but is a show-stopper when in bloom. It too dies back to the ground, but in moderately hardy areas, you may want to take cuttings before frost hits.

Rose-of-Sharon

Another member of the hibiscus genus is the common, old-fashioned Rose-of-Sharon or althea, Hibiscus syriacus. This deciduous shrub can be grown statewide in full sun to partial shade. Single flowers or doubles are available. It blooms from summer through frost, in good soil or bad. While the old fashioned plants were limited to lavender, white or pink flowers, many new selections are available today, with salmon flowers and bi-colors. It blooms on the current season growth, so pruning should be done in late February, prior to new growth beginning. It can be kept in shrub form, or pruned into a small tree.

Regardless of which hibiscus you choose, they all have something to offer, and for the most part, are easy to care for. Most of these plants should be available now at your local nursery. If you need some extra color (and who doesn't) add some hibiscus plants to your collection.

Camellias

When you consider adding flowering shrubs to your landscape, many people consider spring as their primary bloom season, planting azaleas and forsythias. Yet there is a group of plants that can give you flowers from fall through winter, when we desperately need some extra color. Camellias can give you those blooms. While camellias are considered a true southern plant, if given the proper location, they can survive the winters with ease.

Camellias are synonymous with southern gardening, yet they are not native to the south. Originally from China and Japan, there are approximately 65 wild forms of camellias, of which over a dozen forms are in cultivation. In the United States there are three or four commonly grown varieties, or hybrids thereof.

Surprisingly, one of our most common beverages, tea, comes from a camellia - Camellia sinensis. It is one of the leading crops in India and Ceylon, growing up to 50 feet in height. The processed young leaves offer us tea. It is also grown as an ornamental in the deep south, as a much smaller plant, usually 5 - 6 feet. It would need to be brought into a greenhouse or given extra winter protection. There are a few of these plants in the north, but are more common further south. It blooms fragrant white flowers in September and October.

Depending on the variety of camellia, you can have blooms from early fall to early spring. Some varieties are hardier than others, and the further north you live in the state, the more limited you are in selections, and the more winter protection you may need.

Conditions for Growth

Camellias need conditions for growth similar to azaleas, an acid pH, excellent drainage and protection from hot afternoon sun. They grow as an understory plant in their native environment, and therefore, prefer an eastern or northern exposure. They must have some sunlight during the day to set flower buds. They like plenty of moisture, but suffer from root rot in heavy soils or poorly drained soils.

Types

The two most popular types of camellias grown are Camellia japonica, commonly called japonica, and Camellia sasanqua. The japonica varieties are not as winter hardy as the sasanquas.

Japonicas are a zone 8 plant, with a preferred low temperature between 10 and 20 degrees. Sasanquas can tolerate temperatures between 0 and 10 degrees with no damage.

Sasanquas typically bloom earlier than japonicas. Most varieties of sasanquas bloom from mid to late October through early January. Japonica varieties typically begin bloom in early to mid January and continue until spring. Severe winter weather, especially cold winds, may cause some dieback, and can cause flower bud damage on those buds showing color. The bloom period on japonicas is often determined by our winter weather. In mild winters they can begin blooming in early January, and in cold winters it may be delayed until March.

Planting

Japonica varieties will need more protection and benefit from more shade than the sasanquas. They can grow to a height of 15 feet or more. They have a nice pyramidal growth habit and larger leaves, and larger flowers than their counterpart, the sasanqua. Because of their uniform shape, they require little pruning. Give them room to grow to at least 8 to 10 feet.

Repeated heavy pruning can cause damage to the plants. The past few years have shown little winter damage to these plants, but they did suffer heavy damage in the mid-1980's when we had two back-to-back cold winters. Offer them extra protection with sheets, burlap, or Remay, when temperatures are expected below 10 degrees.

Plant camellias on the shallow side, in a well-drained acid soil. Give them plenty of moisture, especially when it is hot and dry. Give them filtered or morning sun, and a little winter protection in extremely cold years, and you will be blessed with a showstopper in your landscape.

Flower Colors

They come in various flower colors, with both single and double blooms, as well as peony, rose and anemone forms. Colors range from white to various shades of pink and red. Some varieties include: 'Bob Hope' with large, semi-double deep red flowers; 'Covina'- semi-double to rose form, rose red blooms; 'Debutante' large peony type flowers, light pink, early bloomer; 'Mathotiana Supreme' extremely large double crimson flower with bright yellow stamens; 'Nuccio's Pearl', double blooms in white petals blushed in a soft orchid pink; 'Nuccio's

Gem' with large double white flowers; and 'Swan Lake', extra large, glistening white blooms.

Camellia Sasanqua

Camellia sasanqua is a more carefree plant. It will tolerate colder temperatures and more sunlight. It is still recommended for a morning sun situation, or filtered light in mid-day. In the north, winter protection will be needed when temperatures fall below zero.

Sasanquas have small glossy leaves, and can grow to a height of 15 feet or more, however most are kept in the six to ten foot range. They have a freer growth habit, and will tolerate more pruning than the japonicas. Since they begin bloom in the fall, they give us some color at a time when other plants have played out. Heavy frosts can damage open blooms, but will not affect the unopened buds, which will open over a period of several weeks.

With ideal conditions, they can be in bloom for 6-8 weeks.

Other Varieties

Probably the most popular variety is 'Yuletide', a brilliant fiery red, single bloom with a bright yellow center. Other varieties include: 'Apple Blossom' white petals with pink edging; 'Bonanza', a semi- double peony form with scarlet blooms; 'Chansonette' brilliant pink, double blooms with ruffled petals; 'Cleopatra', a rose pink, semi-double bloom; 'Usi beni, a pink flower; and White Doves (also called Mine-No-Yuki) with a white semi-double bloom.

Forms

Camellias come in a variety of forms. The most common, of course, is the container with one gallons, three gallons and five gallons available in most cases. Some varieties are available as a 'tree', which means the lower limbs have been pruned off, and it is shaped as a single trunk with the foliage at the top. Other varieties come espaliered, where they are grown one-dimensionally on a trellis. While these are quite attractive, they do require more maintenance, than the traditional potted forms.

Fertilization Needs

Camellias are not heavy feeders. They can be fertilized once a year in the spring with an azalea/camellia food. If the pH gets too high around these plants, they will show signs of iron chlorosis, just like azaleas. This can be prevented by maintaining an acid pH, or corrected with iron chelate. Any pruning which is needed should be done in the spring, after all blooms are gone, and when new growth has begun. But pruning should be kept to a minimum if possible. Also like azaleas, they occasionally will suffer from leaf galls, the waxy-like deformed leaves in cool, wet springs. This is more of a nuisance than a life-threatening disease.

LANDSCAPE CONSTRUCTION

Although most people evaluate the success of a landscape development in terms of the selection and condition of the plant materials, most really well-designed landscapes contain a good balance of construction and plant materials.

Carefully designed and executed paved surfaces, fences, walls, overhead structures and edging materials are not only attractive but also reduce routine maintenance. If possible, when selecting building materials for the landscape, repeat materials and colors already used on the home. Weathered wood, natural stains, concrete and earth tones in brick will usually blend with existing construction materials and relate to the natural environment.

Accessories

Landscape accessories are details which may have no functional purpose, such as surfacing or enclosure, but do have definite visual effects. Accessories also help express individual tastes and preferences. Major accessories, however, should not be afterthoughts; they should be planned as the design evolves.

Accessories add character and dimension to a garden, but poorly selected and placed accessories may spoil an otherwise well-designed landscape.

Many landscape accessories are available. Much of what is available, however, has little or no aesthetic value. To determine whether or not to use an accessory in the garden, ask yourself these questions: (1) Does it have practical use? (2) Is it beautiful in itself? (3) Does it fit or relate to the overall landscape design? Probably the most important of these three questions is the last one.

Garden furniture offers a real opportunity to add utility, color and beauty to the landscape. Comfortable and attractive items are now available in a wide variety of low maintenance outdoorfurniture.Outdoor furniture must be large enough to be practical and must be in scale with its surroundings. Built-in furniture has the added value of being permanently in place and enhancing the overall design. Occasionally the surface of a retaining wall or raised planter can serve as a seating area. The living terrace is the most usual place for outdoor furniture. An interesting piece of driftwood, tree roots or limbs, boulders or rocks provide interesting substitutes for good sculpture. These items are easily blended with the design and may be readily available.

Birdbaths are often used in home landscapes. To be useful they should be shallow, not exceeding 1 1/2 inches in depth, and contain fresh water. Bird houses and feeders should also be selected on the criteria discussed earlier.

Other accessories, such as stained glass, relief sculpture, outdoor chandeliers and plant containers are finding their way into the well-designed landscape. A stained glass window, partially enclosed in an outdoor area, or a burning outdoor chandelier may be added for interest, illumination and possible insect-repelling qualities. Hanging or conventional container plants can add a great deal of interest. With the current trend to return to natural materials and handmade workmanship there is an almost limitless variety of accessories available for our use. The temptation to "overdo" has never been greater. Like other fine things, garden accessories should be used with considerable restraint.

Outdoor lighting can add a great deal to the attractiveness and usefulness of the landscape. Specialists often recommend two separate lighting systems: one for functional and safety purposes and another designed to be beautiful and interesting. Dimmers, low voltage units and other special lighting equipment have become popular and add versatility to outdoor lighting. When placing outdoor lighting for beauty only the effects of lighting should be seen; the source or fixtures are usually hidden in the ground or in tree branches.

Good landscaping is a major investment in time and money. Many people feel that they obtain double enjoyment by including well- designed outdoor lighting to increase the hours of pleasure from their outdoor environment.

TERRACING

Use terraces to make flower and vegetable gardening possible on steep slopes, or simply to add interest to your landscape.

In your backyard

Terraces can create several mini-gardens in your backyard. On steep slopes, terracing can make planting a garden possible. Terraces prevent erosion by shortening the long slope into a series of shorter, more level steps. This allows heavy rains to soak into the soil rather than run off and cause erosion.

Materials for terraces

Numerous materials are available for building terraces. Treated wood is often used because of several advantages: it is easy to work with, blends well with plants, and is often less expensive than other materials. There are many types of treated wood on the market - from railroad ties to landscaping timbers. These materials will last for years. While there has been some concern about using these treated materials around plants, studies have concluded that these materials are not harmful to gardens or people when used as recommended.

Other materials for terraces include bricks, rocks, concrete blocks, and similar masonry materials. Some masonry materials are made specifically for walls and terraces and can be more easily installed by a homeowner than other materials such as field stone and brick. Most stone or masonry products tend to be more expensive than wood.

Height of walls

The steepness of the slope often dictates wall height. Make the terraces in your yard high enough so the land between them is fairly level. Be sure the terrace material is strong enough and anchored well enough to stay in place through freezing and thawing, and heavy rainstorms. Do not underestimate the pressure of water-logged soil behind a wall. It can be enormous and cause improperly constructed walls to bulge or collapse. Many communities have building codes for walls and terraces.

Large projects will need the expertise of a professional to make sure the walls can stand up to water pressure in the soil. Large terraces also need to be built with proper drainage and to be tied back into the slope properly. Because of the expertise and equipment required to do this correctly, you will probably want to restrict terraces you build yourself to no more than a foot or two high.

Building a terrace

The safest way to build a terrace is probably the cut and fill method. With this method, little soil is disturbed, giving you protection from erosion should a sudden storm occur while the work is in progress. This method will also require little, if any, additional soil.

Contact your utility companies to identify the location of any buried utilities before starting to excavate.

Determine the rise and run of your slope. The rise is the vertical distance from the bottom of the slope to the top. The run is the horizontal distance between the top and bottom. This will help you determine how many terraces you need. For example, if your run is 20 feet and the rise is 8 feet and you want each bed to be 5 feet wide, you will need 4 beds. The rise of each bed will be 2 feet.

Start building beds at the bottom of your slope. You will need to dig a trench in which to place your first tier. The depth and width of the trench will vary depending on how tall the terrace will be and the specific building materials you are using. Follow the manufacturer's instructions carefully when using masonry products. Many of these have limits to the number of tiers or the height that can be safely built. If using landscape timbers and your terrace is low (less than 2 feet), you only need to bury the timber to about half its thickness or less.

The width of the trench should be slightly wider than your timber. Make sure the bottom of the trench is firmly packed and completely level. Place your timbers in the trench.

For the sides of your terrace, dig a trench into the slope. The bottom of this trench must be level with the bottom of the first trench. When the depth of the trench is one inch greater than the thickness of your timber, you have reached the back of the terrace and can stop digging.

Cut a timber to the correct length and place in trench.

Drill holes through your timbers and pound long spikes or pipes through the holes and into the ground. A minimum of 18 inches pipe length is recommended; longer pipes may be needed for stability for higher terraces.

Place the next tier of timbers on top of the first, overlapping corners and joints. Spike these together.

Move soil from the back of the bed to the front of the bed until the surface is level. Add another tier as needed.

Repeat, starting with step 2. In continuously connected terrace systems, the first timber of the second tier will also be the back wall of your first terrace.

The back wall of the last bed will be level with the front wall of that bed.

When finished, plant and mulch. Other options for slopes

If terraces are beyond the limits of your time or money, you may want to consider other options for backyard slopes. If you have a slope that is hard to mow, consider using groundcovers other than grass. There are many plants adapted to a wide range of light and moisture conditions that require little care, but provide soil erosion protection.

These include:

Juniper (Juniperus horizontalis) Pachysandra (Pachysandra terminalis) Wintercreeper (Euonymus fortunei) Periwinkle (Vinca minor)

Cotoneaster (Cotoneaster spp.) Potentilla (Potentilla spp.)

Partridge berry (Gaultheria procumbens) Heathers and heaths

Stripcropping is another way to deal with long slopes. Rather than terracing to make garden beds level, plant perennial beds and strips of grass across the slope. Once established, many perennials are effective in reducing erosion. Mulch also helps reduce erosion. The erosion that may occur will be primarily limited to the garden area.

The grass strips will act as filter strips and catch much of the soil that may run off the beds. Grass strips should be wide enough to mow across the hill easily as well as wide enough to effectively reduce erosion.

BACKYARD PONDS

A pond or water garden will likely become the focal point for all your backyard conservation.

Backyard ponds and water gardens are for birds, butterflies, frogs, fish, and you and your family. These ponds are typically small, sometimes no larger than 3 to 4 feet in diameter. They may be built in barrels or other patio containers. Water is effective in drawing wildlife to your backyard. It is also a natural, relaxing, and scenic addition that can provide interest and enjoyment.

Where to put a backyard pond

Consider locating your backyard pond where you can see it from a deck or patio. Have it blend in with its natural surroundings. Elevate the soil around the pond slightly so that excess water will flow away from the pond, not into it. Make sure that any drainage from the pond is away from your house. Plan to landscape around the pond to provide habitat for frogs and birds that need land and water. If you plan to use a pump to recirculate water, use a filter, or light the area, be sure electrical service is available. There will be less maintenance if your pond is not under trees. Most aquatic plants will grow better in full sun.

If you do not have space in your yard for a built-in earthen pond, consider a "tub" pond or large water bowls. These can be placed on the patio and provide many of the same benefits as a built-in pond. There are numerous tub kits available that can be as simple as adding water, a pump, and some plants. They can also be moved inside in the winter as long as good lighting is provided for plants.

Pond liners

Pond liners keep water from seeping into the soil. Even in heavy clay soils, a liner is necessary. You can buy rigid pond liners in a variety of shapes. These are durable and may include built-in waterfalls. Many are quite small. If you want a larger pool or would like to design your own shape, consider using a polyvinyl chloride (PVC) liner. Use a liner specifically designed for pools. While other plastics initially may be cheaper, many are not resistant to ultraviolet light and will break down quickly. Some plastics may also be toxic to fish. Liners also come in different thicknesses. A thicker liner tends to be more resistant to punctures. While expensive and requiring more expertise to install, cement is also an option as a pool liner.

If you use PVC, you will need to get a liner large enough for your pool. To determine how large a piece you will need, determine the maximum width, length, and depth of your pond. Multiply the maximum depth by

Then add this number to both the length and width. This will allow enough plastic to be securely held down around all pond edges.

Installing the pond

You can put in a backyard pond anytime the ground is not frozen or overly wet. If using a pre-formed liner, dig a hole to the correct depth and slightly wider. Insert the liner, making sure it is level and sits securely in the ground. Backfill around the sides. Add water, pump, and plants. Complete landscaping around the pool.

If you use a PVC liner, plan on at least a weekend to install and landscape.

Steps to install a pond with a PVC liner:

Decide on your pond's location.

Using a hose or rope, lay out the shape of your pond on the ground.

Once you are happy with the shape, start digging. Stockpile your topsoil so you can use it to landscape around your pond.

Plan for part of your pond being at least 18 to 24 inches deep; 24 to 36 inches is even better. This will allow for a greater diversity of plants and fish to live in the pond. You may want to make tiers around the inside of the pond at various depths on which to place pots of different aquatic plants. Make tiers about 12 inches wide to accommodate the pots.

Remove any rocks from the excavated area.

To help prevent punctures in the plastic, put a one-inch layer of damp sand on the bottom of the excavated area.

Spread the plastic liner over the hole. Let it sag gently in the hole. Place a few rocks or bricks around the edge to hold in place.

Slowly start filling your pond. The weight of the water will help smooth out the liner. Remove rocks holding the edges to allow liner to conform to the edges of the hole. Smooth out wrinkles but do not pull too tightly. You can walk on the liner if you remove your shoes.

Finish off the pond by placing rocks around the edge to securely hold the liner in place.

Install pump and filter, if desired. Many smaller pumps have a built-in filter. For larger pools, a separate pump and filter may be necessary. Make sure the filter and pump are adequate for the volume of water in your pond. Pumps not only add interest, but are important in adding oxygen to the water. If you want a fountain or waterfall in your pond, you will need a pump to circulate the water.

Let the pond sit for a few days before adding fish and plants. This allows chlorine to evaporate from the water. Chemicals are also available that will quickly neutralize chlorine and other harmful compounds.

Place plants at various depths and add fish.

Establishing plants

For ponds, consider a mix of emergent, submergent, and floating species. Emergent plants, those that have their roots in the water but their shoots above water, can be added to the margins of pools. These include cattails (Typha spp.), arrowhead (Sagittaria spp.), and water lilies (Nymphaea spp.). Submergent species, or those that remain under water such as elodea, are often used as oxygenators. These are plants that remove carbon dioxide from the water and add oxygen.

These plants are essential in most ponds to keep the water clear. Floating species or those that are not anchored at all in the pond include plants such as duckweed (Lemna minor), water lettuce (Pistia stratiotes), and water hyacinth (Eichhornia crassipes). While attractive, water hyacinth and water lettuce can be serious weed problems in the south; however, since they are not winter hardy, there is no problem with them spreading in northern climates.

While not as effective as oxygenators, these plants help keep the water clear by limiting the amount of sunlight that algae receive. In tiny ponds created in barrels and similar containers, these plants may be adequate to maintain clear water.

Choosing and establishing plants for ponds

Consider the following when selecting plants.

How deep is the water? This will be a factor in establishing plants and their survival over winter if you live in colder regions. Some species need a minimum depth of 2 to 3 feet to grow well.

Is your pond permanently installed in the ground or is it a small tub that will be moved inside in the winter? In this case, even tropical plants may be an option.

Will you drain your pond in the winter? If you intend to drain your pond, you should consider plants that can spend the winter in a basement in a dormant state.

How much sunlight does your pond receive?

How large is your pond? If your pond is small, consider dwarf species.

Purchase plants from a reliable vendor. Remember to include some oxygenator plants such as elodea.

Emergent and submergent plants should be planted into pots. A wide assortment of pots is available, from plastic baskets to pulp planters. Choose pots that are large enough for your plants.

If using baskets with numerous perforations, line the basket with burlap or 2 layers of newspaper to keep the soil from falling out of the holes.

Fill the container about half full with a mixture of good garden topsoil. Do not use potting mixes or peat moss. These are too light and will float out of the pot. Adding aquatic plant fertilizer to this bottom layer of soil is recommended for some species. Follow directions on the label for amount.

Place the plant on top of the soil and fill the container with topsoil within one inch of the top.

When planting water lily rhizomes, make a mound of soil in the middle of the pot. Place the rhizome at a 45 degree angle. The crown of the rhizome should be toward the center of the pot. Cover the roots with soil, but not the crown.

In all cases, add a layer of gravel to the top of the pot. This will help keep the soil from floating out and prevent fish from digging in the soil.

Slowly place the pots in the pool to keep soil from floating out. Place pots on bricks to get the desired height.

Floating species can be placed directly into the pond with no other care needed.

Plants should cover 50 to 70 percent of the water surface. Native plants usually do not need fertilizer. For some exotic water lilies, limited fertilizing once yearly may be required. Check with your nursery on care of plants and how deep to place potted plants. Be aware that overfertilizing may cause unwanted algae blooms which can rob the water of oxygen.

Add fish and scavengers

Consider stocking your backyard pond with native fish. They are fun to watch and help keep the pond free of unwanted insects. Most small ponds will warm up quickly in the summer, so make sure you stock with fish that can tolerate elevated temperatures.

You'll also need scavengers, such as aquatic snails and tadpoles, to help control algae. In cold climates, a heater may be necessary for fish to survive the winter. However, this uses a significant amount of electricity and, in most cases, probably is not justified. A better option may be to set up an indoor aquarium in which to overwinter fish and plants.

Maintenance

Algae is a common problem in many newly established ponds. The water often becomes an unsightly green after a few days. While your first instinct is to drain the pond and start over, this only prolongs the problem. Once a pond is "balanced," algae usually are kept at an acceptable level. A balanced pond is one in which the nutrients are at the appropriate level for the plants present. Excess nutrients and light are needed for algae. Reducing the nutrients and decreasing the amount of light entering the water will help reduce algae. Floating plants or those with broad leaves such as water lilies will help reduce the amount of light available for algae and compete for available nutrients. Scavengers such as snails will help clean up wastes from the bottom of the pond.

Pond filters can help reduce algae, but require maintenance. Filters need to be cleaned frequently if algae is a problem. Chemicals can also be used to control algae. Use cautiously as they can be toxic to other plants and aquatic life. The need for algaecides should decrease as plants become established.

Excessive plant growth, especially of free-floating plants, may be a problem. Periodically skim off excess growth of duckweed, water lettuce, and other floating plants. Monthly, prune dying plant material. Clean out some of the decaying plant material that has accumulated in the bottom of the pond in the spring. Remember: a natural pond is not a swimming pool and too much cleaning can do more harm than good.

Safety

Locate the backyard pond where it is unlikely to attract unattended children. Check local safety ordinances to determine if a fence is required for the specific depth and size of your pond.

Check local building ordinances for depth and safety restrictions and permits. Equip outdoor outlets with a ground-fault circuit interrupter. Unplug the pump before cleaning the filter.

LANDSCAPING FOR ENERGY SAVINGS

Are you looking for cost-effective yet eye-pleasing ways to lower your energy bills? Planting trees, shrubs, vines, grasses, and hedges could be the answer. In fact, landscaping may be your best long-term investment for reducing heating and cooling costs, while also bringing other improvements to your community.

Landscaping is a natural and beautiful way to keep your home more comfortable and reduce your energy bills. In addition to adding aesthetic value and environmental quality to your home, a well-placed tree, shrub, or vine can deliver effective shade, act as a windbreak, and reduce overall energy bills.

A well-designed landscape will:

Cut your summer and winter energy costs dramatically. Protect your home from winter wind and summer sun.

Reduce consumption of water, pesticides, and fuel for landscaping and lawn maintenance.

Help control noise and air pollution. Landscaping Saves Money Year-Round Carefully positioned trees can save up to 25% of a household's energy consumption for heating and cooling. Computer models devised by the U.S. Department of Energy predict that the proper placement of only three trees will save an average household between $100 and $250 in energy costs annually.

On average, a well-designed landscape provides enough energy savings to return your initial investment in less than 8 years. An 8-foot (2.4-meter) deciduous (leaf-shedding) tree, for example, costs about as much as an awning for one large window and can ultimately save your household hundreds of dollars in reduced cooling costs, yet still admit some winter sunshine to reduce heating and lighting costs.

Landscaping can save you money in summer or winter.

Summer

You may have noticed the coolness of parks and wooded areas compared to the temperature of nearby city streets. Shading and evapotranspiration (the process by which a plant actively moves and releases water vapor) from trees can reduce surrounding air temperatures as much as 9 degrees F (5 degrees C). Because cool air settles near the ground, air temperatures directly under trees can be as much as 25 degrees F (14 degrees C) cooler than air temperatures above nearby blacktop. Studies by the Lawrence Berkeley Laboratory found summer daytime air temperatures to be 3 degrees F to 6 degrees F (2 degrees C to 3 degrees C) cooler in tree- shaded neighborhoods than in treeless areas.

A well-planned landscape can reduce an unshaded home's summer air- conditioning costs by 15% to 50%. One Pennsylvania study reported air-conditioning savings of as much as 75% for small mobile homes.

Winter

You may be familiar with wind chill. If the outside temperature is 10 degrees F (-12 degrees C) and the wind speed is 20 miles per hour (32 kilometers per hour), the wind chill is -24 degrees F (-31 degrees C).

Trees, fences, or geographical features can be used as windbreaks to shield your house from the wind.

A study in South Dakota found that windbreaks to the north, west, and east of houses cut fuel consumption by an average of 40%. Houses with windbreaks placed only on the windward side (the side from which the wind is coming) averaged 25% less fuel consumption than similar but unprotected homes. If you live in a windy climate, your well-planned landscape can reduce your winter heating bills by approximately one-third.

Landscaping for a Cleaner Environment

Widespread tree planting and climate-appropriate landscaping offer substantial environmental benefits. Trees and vegetation control erosion, protect water supplies, provide food, create habitat for wildlife, and clean the air by absorbing carbon dioxide and releasing oxygen.

The National Academy of Sciences (NAS) estimates that urban America has 100 million potential tree spaces (i.e., spaces where trees could be planted). NAS further estimates that filling these spaces with trees and lightening the color of dark, urban surfaces would result in annual energy savings of 50 billion kilowatt-hours -25% of the 200 billion kilowatt-hours consumed every year by air conditioners in the United States. This would reduce electric power plant emissions of carbon dioxide by 35 million tons (32 million metric tons) annually and save users of utility-supplied electricity $3.5 billion each year (assuming an average of $0.07 per kilowatt-hour).

Also, some species of trees, bushes, and grasses require less water than others. Some species are naturally more resistant to pests, so they require less pesticides. Another alternative to pesticides is integrated pest management, an emerging field that uses least-toxic pest control strategies. One example is to introduce certain insects such as praying mantises or ladybugs to feed on - and limit populations of - landscape-consuming pests.

Certain grasses, such as buffalo grass and fescue, only grow to a certain height - roughly 6 inches (15 centimeters) and are water thrifty. By using these species, you can eliminate the fuel, water, and time consumption associated with lawn mowing, watering, and trimming. Also, recent studies have found that gasoline-powered mowers, edge trimmers, and leaf blowers contribute to air pollution.

Climate, Site, and Design Considerations Climate

The United States can be divided into four approximate climatic regions: temperate, hot-arid, hot-humid, and cool. The energy-conserving landscape strategies you use should depend on which region you live in. These landscaping strategies are listed by region and in order of importance below.

Temperate

Maximize warming effects of the sun in the winter. Maximize shade during the summer.

Deflect winter winds away from buildings. Funnel summer breezes toward the home.

Hot-Arid

Provide shade to cool roofs, walls, and windows.

Allow summer winds to access naturally cooled homes. Block or deflect winds away from air-conditioned homes.

Hot-Humid

Channel summer breezes toward the home.

Maximize summer shade with trees that still allow penetration of low-angle winter sun.

Avoid locating planting beds close to the home if they require frequent watering.

Cool

Use dense windbreaks to protect the home from cold winter winds. Allow the winter sun to reach south-facing windows.

Shade south and west windows and walls from the direct summer sun, if summer overheating is a problem.

Microclimate

The climate immediately surrounding your home is called its microclimate. If your home is located on a sunny southern slope, it may have a warm microclimate, even if you live in a cool region. Or, even though you live in a hot-humid region, your home may be situated in a comfortable microclimate because of abundant shade and dry breezes. Nearby bodies of water may increase your site's humidity or decrease its air temperature.

Your home's microclimate may be more sunny, shady, windy, calm, rainy, snowy, moist, or dry than average local conditions. These factors all help determine what plants may or may not grow in your microclimate.

Siting and Design

A well-oriented and well-designed home admits low-angle winter sun, rejects overhead summer sun, and minimizes the cooling effect of winter winds. If you are building a home, pay attention to its orientation.

In the northern hemisphere, it is usually best to align the home's long axis in an east-west direction. The home's longest wall with the most window area should face south or southeast. The home's north-facing and west-facing walls should have fewer windows because these walls generally face winter's prevailing winds. North-facing windows receive little direct sunlight.

You may be able to design and orient your new house to maximize your homesite's natural advantages and mitigate its disadvantages. Notice your homesite's exposure to sun, wind, and water. Also note the location and proximity of nearby buildings, fences, water bodies, trees, and pavement - and their possible climatic effects. Buildings provide shade and windbreak. Fences and walls block or channel the wind. Water bodies moderate temperature but increase humidity and produce glare. Trees provide shade, windbreaks, or wind channels.

Pavement reflects or absorbs heat, depending on whether its color is light or dark.

If your home is already built, inventory its comfort and energy problems, then use the following landscaping ideas to help minimize these problems.

Shading

Solar heat passing through windows and being absorbed through the roof is the major reason for air-conditioner use. Shading is the most cost-effective way to reduce solar heat gain and cut air-conditioning costs. Using shade effectively requires you to know the size, shape, and location of the moving shadow that your shading device casts.

Remember that homes in cool regions may never overheat and may not require shading.

Trees can be selected with appropriate sizes, densities, and shapes for almost any shading application. To block solar heat in the summer but let much of it in during the winter, use deciduous trees. To provide continuous shade or to block heavy winds, use evergreen trees or shrubs.

Deciduous trees with high, spreading crowns (i.e., leaves and branches) can be planted to the south of your home to provide maximum summertime roof shading. Trees with crowns lower to the ground are more appropriate to the west, where shade is needed from lower afternoon sun angles. Trees should not be planted on the southern sides of solar- heated homes in cold climates because the branches of these deciduous trees will block some winter sun.

A 6-foot to 8-foot (1.8-meter to 2.4-meter) deciduous tree planted near your home will begin shading windows the first year. Depending on the species and the home, the tree will shade the roof in 5 to 10 years. If you have an air conditioner, be aware that shading the unit can increase its efficiency by as much as 10%.

Trees, shrubs, and groundcover plants can also shade the ground and pavement around the home. This reduces heat radiation and cools the air before it reaches your home's walls and windows. Use a large bush or row of shrubs to shade a patio or driveway. Plant a hedge to shade a sidewalk. Build a trellis for climbing vines to shade a patio area.

Vines can shade walls during their first growing season. A lattice or trellis with climbing vines, or a planter box with trailing vines, shades the home's perimeter while admitting cooling breezes to the shaded area.

Shrubs planted close to the house will fill in rapidly and begin shading walls and windows within a few years. However, avoid allowing dense foliage to grow immediately next to a home where wetness or continual humidity are problems. Well-landscaped homes in wet areas allow winds to flow around the home, keeping the home and its surrounding soil reasonably dry.

Wind Protection

Properly selected and placed landscaping can provide excellent wind protection, which will reduce heating costs considerably. Furthermore, these benefits will increase as the trees and shrubs mature. The best windbreaks block wind close to the ground by using trees and shrubs that have low crowns.

Evergreen trees and shrubs planted to the north and northwest of the home are the most common type of windbreak. Trees, bushes, and shrubs are often planted together to block or impede wind from ground level to the treetops. Or, evergreen trees combined with a wall, fence, or earth berm (natural or man-made walls or raised areas of soil) can deflect or lift the wind over the home. Be careful not to plant evergreens too close to your home's south side if you are counting on warmth from the winter sun.

A windbreak will reduce wind speed for a distance of as much as 30 times the windbreak's height. But for maximum protection, plant your windbreak at a distance from your home of two to five times the mature height of the trees.

If snow tends to drift in your area, plant low shrubs on the windward side of your windbreak. The shrubs will trap snow before it blows next to your home.

In addition to more distant windbreaks, planting shrubs, bushes, and vines next to your house creates dead air spaces that insulate your home in both winter and summer. Plant so there will be at least 1 foot (30 centimeters) of space between full-grown plants and your home's wall.

Summer winds especially at night can have a cooling effect if used for home ventilation. However, if winds are hot and your home is air conditioned all summer, you may want to keep summer winds from circulating near your home.

www.ingramcontent.com/pod-product-compliance
Ingram Content Group UK Ltd.
Pitfield, Milton Keynes, MK11 3LW, UK
UKHW022212230426
12048UKWH00016BA/797